REDEMPTION SONG

'And I will restore unto you the years that the locust hath eaten. And ye shall praise the Name of the Lord your God that hath dealt wondrously with you.'

JOEL 2:25,26

REDEMPTION SONG

JOE PEDEN

with

JAMES MCCLELLAND

REDEMPTION SONG
First Published 1991

Copyright © Joe Peden 1991

All Rights Reserved

Printed And Published By
AMBASSADOR PRODUCTIONS LTD
Providence House,
16 Hillview Avenue,
Belfast, BT5 6JR,
UK.

ISBN 0 907927 71 8

CONTENTS

Dedicated to the memory of my dear Mother
Charlotte Peden
Who loved to have her family gathered around her.
I pray that all the family will one day gather again with
her

Beyond the sunset
O glad reunion
With our dear loved ones,
Who've gone before
In that fair homeland
We'll know no parting
Beyond the sunset forever more.

To my dear wife Phyllis and our family
Fiona, Samuel and Aaron
Mark and Julia
Janet and Andrew

To my minister Rev. Austin Allan
To my co-author James McClelland
And to all who gave of their time and love
that this book might be written.

1

CROSSROADS

The early light of another dawn ventured in through the chinks in the curtains and touched the eyes of the man who lay sleeping. He hadn't been there very long but as he stirred from his slumber the words of his next door neighbour immediately ran through his mind.

"Do you see you big fella. I'll be over at daylight when you're sober and I'll tell you just what I think of you!"

Joe feared the man who lived next door. Not because of his size, for he was smaller than Joe. He feared him because he knew he was right. He knew that he spoke the truth and his words burned into Joe's heart like a branding iron.

SENSELESS

The night before Joe had been driven home, yet again, absolutely drunk. So drunk that he daren't drive his own car. In fact, so drunk that he hardly knew how to find the way home. His drinking companions had driven him home in the early hours of the morning, parked his car at his gate, and left him sitting in it. The wee man who lived next door had gone out in his pyjamas and carried Joe into the house. Joe was so drunk that he couldn't even sit in the chair but fell on to the floor where he lay in an almost senseless stupor. The commotion awakened Joe's wife and children who came downstairs to investigate. The sight of the head of the house completely overcome by the power of drink brought tears to their eyes.

As he lay there listening to the cries of his family his thoughts went back to his own childhood. His father had been a drunkard too. His mother had been heart-broken almost all her married life. Drink had taken the food from their table; the furniture from their house, the happiness from their home, and ultimately, the home from over their heads. It eventually took Joe's father's life too. And now it seemed as if Joe was determined, even destined, to follow his father's example.

It was as he lay there that the neighbour, the wee man who lived next door, had spoken the words that now struck terror into Joe's heart. The expectation of the wee man coming over to face Joe with the folly of his ways had a wonderfully sobering effect on him.

"It was just like getting a bucket of cold water thrown over me," he recalls.

However, Joe was no simpleton. He had discussed spiritual matters with this man before and he had a fair idea what he would be saying to him. So as he lay there in bed, waiting for his neighbour to call, he made ready his answers. He would know exactly what to say. He would refute every accusation. He wouldn't allow this man to persuade him that what he was doing was wrong, or that it was something that he, Joe Peden, couldn't handle.

But the neighbour never came - and Joe never needed his answers. Instead, the neighbour decided on a different strategy. After he had seen Joe safely put to bed he and his wife sat up for the rest of that night discussing the situation. They decided that to go over next morning and tear into Joe about his drinking habits would probably do more harm than good. They remembered the advice of Jesus, "Be ye wise as serpents and harmless as doves."

And so they decided on an altogether different tack. They would pray! They wouldn't say a word to Joe. After all he couldn't do a thing about his problem. Drink now had the better of him. It was his master and it called the shots. All the scolding in the world, all the logic in the world, all the pleading in the world, wouldn't change Joe. It needed a much greater power. A divine power!

Every day they brought the name of Joe Peden to their Lord in prayer. And they prayed very specifically. They prayed for his salvation.

TERROR

Three weeks later, in the early hours of a Friday morning, Joe came home again the worse for drink. It was after one o'clock in the morning when he stumbled into bed and laid down his head to sleep. But there was no sleep for Joe. And there was to be no sleep for him for a long time.

As soon as his head hit the pillow he began to think. And the subject that filled his thoughts was death. Terror gripped him like a man condemned. He jumped out of bed again and ran down stairs. His wife Phyllis, convinced that something terrible was wrong, ran down the stairs after him. But Joe couldn't explain the troubled state of his mind.

"Come back to bed," Phyllis pleaded. "You'll get something sorted out tomorrow."

But Joe couldn't be persuaded. He was convinced that if he put his head down on the pillow again that night to sleep, he would never wake up.

The reason for his anxiety was not just the fear of death - but what lay beyond it. From childhood Joe had been familiar with the message of the gospel. In Sunday school he had learned the good news that Jesus loved sinners and had died on the cross to save them from sin. But he was also aware of the consequences of disobeying the gospel message. He knew that after death there was certain judgment and he feared the outcome of that judgment. He feared that if he died in his present state he would be lost in Hell forever. Joe was terrified of Hell.

A MAN CONDEMNED

All that night he walked the floor of his living room. He could find no peace in anything. He did the same thing all the next day - and all the next night. Right through till Saturday morning he paced back and forth like a man condemned. He didn't know who to turn to, or what to do. But of one thing he was sure. He couldn't live like this anymore. He couldn't explain his plight to his wife either, and she, almost as distressed as Joe was, could offer him neither hope nor solace.

"I'm going out," he said. "I don't know where I'm going and I don't know when I'll be back."

He made his way into Tandragee where he met his brother Jim. Jim had been saved a few weeks earlier and as Joe poured out his heart to him, he understood - and he knew what to do. Stopping Joe in his tracks he said, "I'll take you to see a man who'll be able to help you."

If this man could help Joe Peden it would be the turning point in a life that seemed almost destined to ruination - from birth!

2

EARLY DAYS

The darkness above the city of Belfast was pierced only by the powerful searchlights that probed the night sky. The constant drone of German aircraft was persistently interrupted by the steady firing of anti aircraft guns. Every now and then the faint whistle, as a bomb was released and began dropping, was followed by a distant explosion, as the bomb found its target.

It was the night of the 6th April 1944. As the German bombers emptied their weapons of death over East Belfast, aiming for the nearby aircraft factory and ship-yard, in a little terrace house in Parkgate Avenue new life was coming forth. Charlotte Peden was giving birth to her fourth child, a boy. Joe was the second boy in the family and there were also two girls.

In the providence of God the Peden home was spared that night. Indeed, it was spared throughout the length of the war. However, in due course the little terraced house in East Belfast became too small for them and a move was necessary. They went to Ballygowan for a short time and then to a brand new house in the Cregagh Estate.

THE DEMON DRINK!

Joe can't remember a time when drink wasn't a problem in their house. From his earliest days he remembers his father coming in at night drunk. It was a house that hardly ever knew peace and happiness when the father was about. In his drunkenness he would vent his anger on his wife and children. Many a time Charlotte Peden felt the might of his fists as he struck her physically. At the same time he struck emotional terror into the hearts of his children.

Robert Peden's drinking habits brought serious financial difficulties to his family. They had a lovely house, perfect for the growing family, but no matter how Mrs. Peden balanced the books there was never enough to feed and clothe her children as well as pay the rent. She tried very hard but, eventually, they had to leave for a smaller place, in Coburg Street, just off the Woodstock Road.

The move was only temporary. The father's drinking habits continually worsened and there was even less money than before. Joe's mother found herself continually asking for credit. When it came to providing for her family she was a miracle worker. Her supply was always meagre but somehow or other she could always eke it out. One cousin remembers Aunt Lottie as being a woman who could have, "Prepared a banquet, literally, from nothing." I suppose these skills were hard learned and of necessity. However, great as her housekeeping skills undoubtedly were, they couldn't prevent the family from the further shame of another eviction.

FAMILY BREAK UP

The constant strain of trying to provide for her young family in such circumstances took its eventual toll on Charlotte Peden's health. She was in a totally run down condition due to the immense strain she'd been under for years and the unexpected outcome of it all was admission to hospital.

With the mother gone and the father incapable of looking after the children there was only one solution. The family would have to be split up. Some were taken to stay with relatives and the rest, one of them being Joe, were placed in care, in "Glen-dew" children's hostel.

Joe has happy memories of the hostel. There was always plenty of food, a happy atmosphere, kind and considerate staff and no daddy coming home at night, drunk and abusive. This was a much better environment for a little boy to grow up in. It wasn't to last, however, for as soon as Mrs. Peden was discharged from hospital, she was keen to gather her family about her again. However hard the circumstances, she would have her children with her and they would face the future together.

The next few months were spent to-ing and fro-ing between a couple of relatives homes while proper housing was sought and sorted out. All this brought affairs at home to a head and Joe's mother decided to gather up her children and take them off to the country - to Tandragee, in County Armagh.

A NEW LIFE

I suppose there comes a time in the life of almost any woman, living under such strain, when it becomes impossible to go on any more. It's more important to get the children into an environment where they'll have some chance of normality, than to try and preserve the family unit.

Charlotte Peden had had enough of the present life style, so she decided to up stakes and strike out for a new life. Without any announcement to the father and without leaving any kind of message or forwarding address, the children were bundled onto the bus one day and the next stop was Tandragee.

They stayed at first with relatives, but after a week or two, they got a wee house in Mill Row. How Joe's mother paid the rent he still doesn't know, but somehow the miracle worker did it again.

Just around this time Joe's father, Robert, caught up with them again. Some sort of reconciliation was effected and he came to live with them in Mill Row. By this time the drink had taken it's toll on him and his health suffered badly. In fact he never worked again.

SCHOOL-DAYS

Joe has good memories of growing up in Tandragee. The new surroundings; the wide open spaces and the fresh country air all had a good effect on him. Life was much better here - except for one thing - school.

Joe's memories of school are not so good and yet there's no reason why they shouldn't be. He was above average intelligence. He didn't find study difficult. In fact, he was one of those fortunate people who seemed not to need very much study to do well. His school work was always good and he regularly came out top of the class in tests and exams.

His work was so good that the headmaster felt Joe had every chance of going on to grammar school. He thought Joe should enter for the qualifying examination and he sent Joe's mother several letters to that effect. However, he made one cardinal mistake. He made Joe the postman. Joe opened the letters and when he read the contents, the letters were discarded. Mrs. Peden never saw them. Joe had no intention of spending one day more at school that was absolutely necessary.

In common with thousands of other wee lads, he hated the place. He didn't have any interest in academic advance. There were other things that, at that age, were far more important to him. Like football!

FOOTBALL CRAZY!

"He's football crazy, he's football mad."

The words of that old song could certainly be applied to young Joe Peden. He just lived for the game and dreamed of one day becoming a star of the turf. This went back to his earliest childhood days in East Belfast where he lived, for a time, beside the Oval football ground, the home of Glentoran.

"As a young boy I used to watch the Glens and I idolised them. I suppose as all young boys do I always dreamed dreams that one day I would be a footballer. That was the burning ambition of my life."

He seemed to have been built for the sport. He was tall, lithe, supple and had been blessed with what a goalie needs most - a generous pair of hands. And he was fearless! It didn't matter how fast a ball came at him, he would go for it, and most times he stopped it. He was so good at the game and so valuable to the school team that, even when he mitched school, the headmaster would send for him to play on those evenings when the school team was in competition.

So it's not surprising that his fascination for the game interfered with his schooling. In years to come football was to play an even bigger part in his life and to have more of an influence than he ever dreamed. But for the moment he had to face up to the reality that, from Monday to Friday, the school room and the school books beckoned.

As time wore on Joe's interest in things academic grew no better. If the truth be told, it waned. So much so that he hatched a plan to escape the place and if he had kept it to himself he might have got away with it a lot longer than he did. As it happened, for seven whole weeks he never saw the inside of the school house.

"I used to leave the house in the mornings, singing, whistling and smiling. I'm sure my mother wondered why I was suddenly so happy to be going off to school."

If she did she never showed any hint of being suspicious and it would appear that she never had any inkling that anything was wrong.

Joe dressed, packed his bag and set off for school every morning at the usual time. He made his way up the main street in Tandragee in the general direction of the school. However, when he got to the top of the town, instead of turning right and continuing on towards school, he turned left, crossed the road and slipped in under the big gate that marked the main entrance to the castle grounds.

Inside, the demesne was a wonderful place. A maze of narrow paths or tracks led off the one main drive. Trees and shrubs grew in abundance, so it was a real adventure playground for a boy of eleven.

On one day Joe was a cowboy, tracking the Indians. On another an explorer looking for some hidden treasure from the past. On another a soldier in the deepest jungles of a far off land. There were trees to climb, potatoes to roast over the open flame of a camp fire and, if the weather turned nasty, you could always sit beneath the branches of a spreading oak and smoke a Woodbine. It was a real Tom Sayer existence and Joe loved it.

For forty-nine consecutive days Joe lived this marvellous life of a truant. It could probably have gone on a lot longer if he hadn't been so eager to share it with others. On that last fateful day he met another lad on the way up the street and managed to persuade him of the benefits of this life of freedom.

Whether Joe was a super salesman, or whether the other lad was equally disenchanted with school we'll never know. Anyway, by the time they both reached the top of the town Joe had persuaded him to follow the dream and together they slipped below the castle gate into their world of adventure.

Unknown to them, a little old lady who lived beside the Pedens, caught sight of them as they disappeared into the estate. It didn't take her very long to bring the news home to the two mothers. And it didn't take much longer for them to go into action with a counter plan. Before that day ended Joe would experience the reality of a truth he was to learn years later. "Be sure your sin will find you out!"

"The sun was shining. It was a lovely day and this other lad and I were walking along through the grounds singing at the tops of our voices,

'I love to go a wandering along the mountain track,
And as I go I love to sing, my knapsack on my back.'

"However, the singing came to an abrupt end when we turned a corner in one of the paths and were confronted with a sight that struck terror into both of us - our mothers."

Joe's mother was armed with her favourite weapon - the floor brush. There was no time given for any kind of explanation, not that any excuse would have held water.

"I tried to head towards home but she turned me and drove me, the floor brush spinning like the blades of a helicopter, towards school."

Joe was marched up through the town of Tandragee, out the Portadown Road, in through the school gates, into the building, down the corridor, into the class-room - and right into the seat. Only then did his mother speak.

"If you ever do that again I'll kill you!"

Joe never did mitch school again. From that day on he had to put up with it and make the best of it. But he longed for the day when the school bell would ring for him for the last time and he would be free.

However, he does have some good lasting memories of school. Memories which centre around one man in particular.

John Adams was the kind of school-master who would put his hand on your shoulder and try to make you realise that school wasn't such a bad place after all. He had to deal with most of the problems with Joe but he always managed to turn them into an opportunity to encourage the young lad to do better. He took a keen interest in Joe and sought to guide him in the right direction.

"I was once your age too, Joe." Mr. Adams would say.

"I remember those days and I used to enjoy doing the same things that you're doing now."

"Here was a man," thought Joe, "who seems to understand the problems young people face."

However, whilst all this kindness and under-standing from Mr. Adams has left a lasting impression on Joe, to this day, it didn't have very much effect on him at the time. Granted, the severe reprimand at the hands of his mother put an end to his ideas about 'mitching' school again, but it didn't diminish his dislike of the place. He longed for the day when he could say good-bye to it forever.

At last, when he was just fifteen, it came. Joe was almost thankful for the family circumstances which, eventually, allowed him to turn his back on his school-days, forever.

3

GROWING UP

During his latter years at school Joe began to realise just how difficult life was for his mother. His father hadn't worked in years. The family depended, very largely, on social security and the kindness of friends and relatives.

As the older members of the family left school, got work and began bringing in a little money Joe fostered this desire to play his part too. So he used to do odd jobs, and whatever money he earned, he brought it home and gave it to his mother, to help ease the burden.

Once he did leave school he got a job in the local spinning mill. A 'rove boy' had to work hard and there weren't many opportunities for slacking. Joe's job was to supply the spinning room with the huge bobbins of flax which, in turn, were loaded by the women onto the massive spinning frames and turned into finished thread. Eventually they would become tablecloths, place settings, handkerchiefs and bed sheets to grace the homes of the well-to-do in places as far away as Frankfurt, New York and Sydney.

It was tough work, even for a strapping lad in his teens and many a time the sweat rolled down Joe's brow as he pushed the awkward trolleys, piled high with bobbins of flax, from the store room to the spinning floor. What an insatiable appetite these spinning machines had!

After six months of this, 'hard labour,' Joe got a job with an engineering firm at Laurelvale, just outside Tandragee. This was a different type of work and called more for skill than hard graft. In course of time he was able to serve his apprenticeship and became a welder, a trade he has stuck to ever since.

FUN LOVING

He was growing up into well matured, happy young man and like most of the others of his generation, as well as being prepared to work hard for a living, he enjoyed a bit of fun too.

The week-ends were looked forward to with great anticipation. Saturday afternoons saw him on the football field, in serious combat with the opposing team. He would shout himself hoarse as the rest of his own team attacked the opponent's goal and will them on to score. And when his own goal was attacked he would spring into action, diving, jumping and using those big hands to keep the ball safe.

Friday and Saturday nights were times for fun and leisure, and one of the big attractions was the dance hall. In those days groups of young people from the surrounding towns would descend on Tandragee, or Gilford, or Banbridge for a great get together at a dance.

ROMANCE

"It was different in those days to what it is now. Gangs of young people hardly ever met face to face, just for a fight. They met to have fun and to get to know each other better. It was at a night like this, a dance in Tandragee, that I met the girl who later became my wife."

After that Joe and Phyllis began going out together. Their friendship developed into love and eventually they decided to get married. Phyllis belonged to Gilford Presbyterian Church and that's where the wedding was held, in 1964.

"When I look back at the difficult years of our marriage, when I was drinking the bit out, I suppose I have to thank the Lord for giving me the wife he did. Phyllis put up with a lot of things that no other person would have endured. There's an old saying, *'When the Lord made them, he matched them,'* and that's certainly true in my case. Phyllis is one in a million and I thank God for her."

Phyllis was, indeed still is, a woman in a million. She was a good home builder and a great mother to the children. When Joe was in the horrors of drink, week after week, it was Phyllis who carried the burden of the family and held it together.

FOOTBALL!

From his earliest days Joe Peden loved to kick a football. In the tiny streets of East Belfast, where he was born, soccer enjoyed an above average popularity. After all, the Oval football ground, home of the local team, Glentoran, was barely a stone's throw away. Almost every wee lad in the area could see himself as a future Johnny Carey or a Stanley Matthews. Young Joe Peden was no exception.

Joe displayed a natural talent early on, so that, by the time he was in his early teens he was playing with boys much older than himself. Those big hands, the longs arms and that tall, supple body enabled him to go for a ball, no matter where it came from - and no matter how fast. When a striker is taking a penalty kick he puts a lot of power into his shot. That ball comes at the goal-keeper at incredible speed. He needs a lot of concentration and a lot of courage to be in the right place to stop it. Joe Peden was fearless in those situations. He had what is referred to in the soccer world as, *'a safe pair of hands.'*

His ability brought him to the attention of a number of scouts and there were plenty of offers for places in the team. At fifteen he began his serious career with Tandragee Rovers and shortly after that came his first signing. Ballymena United was a "B" division team and even though Joe's place was on the reserve team it was seen as the first stepping stone on a promising football career.

"If you look after yourself Joe, and do the right things there's no reason why you shouldn't go far," he was told by the older and wiser men in the game.

HERO!

Just around that same time another young shining soccer star was coming onto the Irish scene. Pat Jennings, from Newry, was a contemporary of Joe. He too, had a long, lithe body, great speed and a large pair of hands. He and Joe faced each other on opposing teams now and again and Joe remembers him as a gentle, gracious character. Of course, Pat Jennings went on to become a household name in soccer and to be capped for his country many times.

Pat Jennings of course, being around the same age as Joe, was much too young to be any sort of hero in those days, although Joe admires the great heights he has ascended to since then. But Joe had his own hero in those days and he still remembers him with affection..

Harry Gregg was an Irish international and also played in goals for Manchester United. He was one of *"Busby's Babes"* as they called them, after their manager Matt Busby, who had done so much to weld them into the most formidable side in Europe. Gregg was also aboard the ill-fated flight from Munich, on February 6th 1958, when so many great names in soccer lost their lives.

TRAGEDY!

As the team began the last leg of their homeward trip from Belgrade, after qualifying for the European Cup semi-finals, their BEA Ambassador aircraft, after one abortive attempt, set off down the runway, tried to take off, hit a fence and an airport building, and broke in two.

Seven members of that superb squad lost their lives that day, as well as eight journalists covering the match, and three members of the club's staff.

Matt Busby himself, was seriously injured but recovered both in health and courage, to rebuild the team and restore it's pride.

Mercifully, Harry Gregg survived the crash too, and continued his career in football with great success.

Joe Peden remembers exactly where he was when the news of the horrific Munich air disaster broke. Like thousands of other soccer fans he was devastated, and waited anxiously as the full story unfolded, to find out who, precisely, had died that day.

"Manchester United were *the* team of the day. *'Busby's Babes'* were something special, and because my personal hero, Harry Gregg, was a part of that team and on the flight, it was a very emotional day for me," Joe recalls.

DREAMS OF GLORY

"Unless you've played football you can't really understand why young people are so attracted to the sport," he claims.

"There's something that gets you inside when you walk onto that pitch. Every young person wants to be on the winning team. Every young person dreams of playing in a cup final, of displaying his skills at a cup final on that famous turf at Wembley, and of hearing the roar of the crowd when a goal is scored."

"I was substitute on the Glentoran team when we played Glasgow Rangers in the European Cup at Ibrox Park. And to be there in an atmosphere with forty thousand people is something that's hard to imagine - so unbelievable. You couldn't see the crowd through the glare of the floodlights, but you could hear them. It's hard to explain the feeling it gives you. All I can say is that it was electrifying. As a kid you try to imagine what it will be like. But you can't until you're there. It's something special!"

Joe, too, dreamed of Wembley. He dreamed of *"the big one,"* a cup final, with himself in goal,

31

stopping every ball and his team coming out champions.

SUCCESS

But football is tough work if you want to be serious about it. For Joe it meant working hard all day at the engineering firm and then training two nights a week to stay in trim for the games at the week-ends.

He was playing one night at a match in Portadown and the manager of another nearby team, Banbridge Town, was there. He spotted Joe, liked his style and ability and, after the match, approached Joe with an offer to play for the club. This was to be Joe's first signing.

"You have to sign your name to a form which is then forwarded to the Irish Football Association. That makes you a registered player for that team and, of course, you can't then play for any other team."

Amateurs, like Joe, weren't supposed to be paid for their services but it was quite common for players to receive a few pounds every week. That, in itself, was a good incentive and it meant that Joe could further supplement the family income.

Joe continued at Banbridge Town for a few seasons and, eventually, found himself at the Oval, in Belfast, in 1965, playing against Glentoran, in the Irish Cup.

"We played them on a Friday night and I remember the game well. Unfortunately, they beat us four goals to two. Still I had a super game and felt no real disgrace at letting in four of their shots."

In fact the truth is that, but for Joe's goal-keeping skills the result could have been fourteen - two. Glentoran were a powerful team. Banbridge were no match for them, but the overall result did Joe's career no harm.

THE GLENS

At the time the Glens were on the lookout for a new goal-keeper and they wanted Joe to fill the space.

This was a tremendous step up the ladder. Up till now Joe had been playing for a team which was in the middle of the "B" division. All of a sudden he was being propelled into the top team in Ireland.

There was a transfer fee involved and Joe received something in the order of £50, not bad back in those days. But the big money went to the Banbridge Town club.

To this day Joe doesn't know how much they were paid for his release.

However, there were a couple of other perks to come his way. He was guaranteed £5 for every match he played - and another bonus of £2 for a win.

"If I played three or four matches a week I was getting as much as £28. That wasn't bad for a young fellow."

Not bad at all! In fact, Joe was earning a lot more from football than from his engineering job. Any man bringing home £25 a week, back in 1965, was very well paid. It was a very decent living wage. Although he reflects, "I loved the game so much I would have played for nothing."

SWEET 'N SOUR

However, life doesn't always run sweetly and the best of arrangements can turn sour, sometimes as quickly as milk.

A few of the boys who were playing for Glentoran, including Joe, had a bit of a dispute with the club about how they were being treated.

These were country lads and they felt they weren't being given the same courtesies as the other chaps from the city. So they decided to withhold their services. That meant, in effect, that they were out of football till their contracts expired.

They had to sit at home on Saturdays and nurse their frustrations, in the hope that at the end of the time another club would take them on.

Joe was quite fortunate. Once he was a free agent again the Portadown based Glenavon club sought his services and he signed for them.

MEMORIES

Joe looks back on the heady days of his football career with mixed feelings. He's proud to have been part of the whole scene at the time, although nowadays he doesn't even watch soccer on television - not even the cup final.

It's nice to read the headlines and sports stories that were written about him. He gets quite a kick when he leaves through the old scrap-book and reads the glowing reports on the young Tandragee lad who rarely missed a ball. And the action shots of him jumping for a high ball or diving at an attackers feet, bring a certain sense of timeless satisfaction.

"One of the proudest moments was the morning I opened the big brown envelope. It was a letter from the Irish Football Association asking me to report to the International Hotel in Belfast on the following Friday."

The year was 1965 and that invitation took him to the Oval again for a junior international match against Scotland. It was Joe's first cap in the sport and even though they were beaten two - nil, for Joe, it was one of the highlights of his soccer years. He still cherishes the cap, too, and shows it off to friends, with pride.

"I look back now over my years in football and I have to say, it was good, it really was good," he muses.

MOTHER'S PRIDE!

As you would expect, Joe's success at the game brought a great deal of joy and pride to his mother and father. His mother didn't have much interest in going to watch football matches, and his father, now sadly in failing health, wasn't fit to go. However, they both snipped out the press reports on their famous son and compiled a scrap-book. When the relatives and friends came round of an evening there would be a while spent poring over the cuttings of Joe's most recent successes.

It was a more innocent era for sportsmen too. The very idea of a footballer having a drink was unheard of.

"If you were caught with a bottle of beer in your hand, it didn't matter how good you were, you were out."

The social clubs weren't a big part of the football scene back in those days. There wasn't the same temptation and there wasn't the same opportunity. The sad and un-gentlemanly side of football, so regularly a feature of sports news today, was still a thing of the future.

REGRETS

Ah, but there are regrets too. If only he'd been more dedicated. If only he'd realised what opportunities were at his disposal he might have tried even harder - and he might have enjoyed even greater success. But when he's pressed with the question, "Is it something you'd want for your son?" the answer is a very emphatic "No!"

The reason for that is altogether different, but simple. It was football, the thing that was nearest and dearest to him, that led to his eventual downfall and almost ruined him.

The saddest, most horrifying and regrettable days of Joe Peden's life were still to come.

4

WHEN TRAGEDY STRIKES

It's quite amazing how many people have been brought to the place of surrender and dedication to God, through the most trying circumstances of life. It's equally amazing how long it often takes before the voice of God is heard in such circumstances, and men respond.

Joe Peden is no exception to this rule. In the rough game of life he suffered many defeats at the hand of the Lord, before realising that God had much greater rewards for him than the game of soccer could ever offer.

If only he could have seen ahead! What did the roar of an excited football crowd matter, compared to the blessing of multitudes through the singing of a gospel song? What did the stopping of a powerful penalty kick matter, compared to the saving of souls from a lost eternity? And what did fame and fortune in the world of soccer matter, compared to the fellowship of the people of God?

SACRIFICE

For Joe Peden today, God's way is perfect, but it took a long time and a lot of hard training to get him there. Just after he signed for Glenavon, events in his family began to dictate a different pattern to his life.

First, his brother-in-law, was seriously injured in a vehicle accident. He was a driving instructor in the army and also drove the vehicles to demonstrate them to other European countries. During one of these demonstrations, that of an amphibious machine called a *"Stalwart,"* the suspension collapsed and he suffered a broken back.

He was taken to Stoke Mandeville hospital, in London, where he spent the next ten months making a very slow, but only partial recovery. He's still paralysed from the waist down. The family did the only thing a family could do; they gathered round to give whatever support they could.

For Joe, this meant some radical changes to his footballing activities. Every other week-end he and his wife flew over to London to be with the sick man. He needed support, encouragement and above all, company. The accident to her brother had a devastating effect on Phyllis too. She and her brother were very close and it was painful for her to watch her once active brother now reduced to this state. Joe had to try and give an extra measure of support to her.

Her brother has never fully recovered from his injuries. Today he wears callipers on his legs and can move over very short distances by himself. However, unless some miracle takes place, he'll never be what he once was.

All this time spent in London meant that, for Joe, the football took a back seat. He just wasn't available to play on a regular basis.

DEATH

That tragedy had barely been recovered from, when Joe's father was taken into hospital, seriously ill. It was Christmas eve 1969. The life he had led had finally taken it's toll on his health and in a few days the grim news was announced to the family that he had lung cancer.

"It was quite a shock to be told that he was so ill," remembers Joe. "They said he could live for a few months, perhaps a year at the outside. But, in fact, it was all over in three weeks."

Lung cancer's an awful thing and it's quite painful to watch someone, especially someone near and dear to you, die of such a thing. At the same time I suppose it should have been a warning to Joe. His father had been a heavy smoker all his life and it was the cigarettes that finally killed him. And yet, Joe used to sit by his bedside and puff away at cigarettes the whole time. The air around the bed would have been blue with smoke and yet it never dawned on him that what he was doing could put him in that same hospital bed in years to come.

"The sister in the hospital ward used to walk past and say to me, *'Are you so stupid that you can't see what you're doing. Those things have killed you're father. How can you sit there and smoke them too?'"*

Joe's father died on the 9th January 1970 and that had an immediate bad effect on his mother. Even though she'd had a tough thirty-six years with this man, he was her partner in life and there was a bond of love there which cannot be easily broken, if ever.

MOTHER

Even though there was no longer the daily hardship and challenge, Charlotte Peden was broken by the death of her husband. There seemed barely anything to live for anymore and she just, literally, took to her bed.

"We used to remind her of what life was like when my father was alive. The hardship, the misery, the pain. But she didn't seem to remember all that - just that the sweetheart of her youth, the father of her children and the husband of a lifetime was gone."

Thankfully however, with the patient understanding of the family and the help of her own doctor, Mrs. Peden recovered. All of a sudden she noticed that life was easier and she began to get some enjoyment from it. She was able to visit friends and relatives she hadn't seen for years; and she was able to go places she hadn't been to for years. For Joe, it was tremendous to see these changes in his mother's life.

PERSONAL TRAGEDY

But there was still more trouble ahead for Joe, and this of a much more personal nature.

Because he hadn't been playing football regularly for a long time Joe wasn't as fit as he needed to be to take part at the previous higher level. The Glenavon club had kept in touch and still wanted him on their team but he needed to be fully fit. So he started to play some junior soccer again, to get himself in shape and to hone the old skills to their former perfection.

"Thirty-five minutes into the fourth match we played I clashed with another player. As soon as we hit each other a stabbing pain shot right to the top of my head. At the same time there was an unmerciful crack, just like the breaking of a stick."

Joe's leg was broken between the knee and the ankle. It wasn't just the regular fracture either. Both bones of the leg were broken clean in two so that the lower half of the leg and foot lay helplessly at right angles to the upper half.

The match was stopped immediately and the first aid people ran to his aid. There was nothing the doctor could do, except pump an injection of pain killer into him. When the ambulance arrived they took full control, although Joe barely remembers what took place.

HOSPITAL

"They tied the legs together at the knees, lifted me on to the stretcher and into the ambulance. Because the leg was so badly broken it couldn't be straightened and so, all the way to the hospital one of the nurses had to support the lower half of my leg. That ambulance journey from Richill to Lurgan hospital was one of the longest I can remember."

However, the ambulance ride was nothing compared to what was to come. The damage was much worse than was at first realised. The broken bones had pierced out through the skin and the whole lower portion of the leg was in an awful mess.

There were numerous operations, plaster casts, pills and injections - all accompanied by constant pain - and , of course, confinement to bed, twenty fours hours a day.

It had a devastating effect on Joe. He couldn't sleep. He couldn't eat. He couldn't relax. And so he went to the only possible source of comfort he knew.

"I just smoked day and night in hospital. On my locker, on a Sunday afternoon, I would have had almost six hundred cigarettes. Yet I saw me on Tuesday evening waiting on the trolley coming round, so I could buy more."

Smoking at such a rate, of course, had a serious effect on Joe's health. It destroyed his appetite to such an extent that, over the six weeks he was in hospital, he lost two and a half stones in weight. It slowed down the healing process, too, which considerably aggravated the surgeon, a very skilled South African called Mr. Allen. He was continually barging Joe and exhorting him to *"kick"* the habit.

Although Joe couldn't see it, the surgeon was probably right because for eight months the leg was kept in plaster, from the foot to the thigh. Even then, the problems weren't over.

Further surgery followed, with this time the implanting of a stainless steel bar into the leg, from the knee to the ankle.

SHATTERED DREAMS

All this put an end to the promising football career. Mr. Allen, took Joe aside one day and told him that, from now on, any ideas of a return to the soccer pitch would have to be put out of his mind. There was no way that the leg, even when fully healed, would ever stand up to the pressures of kicking a football again.

Joe had saved his last goal - and played his last match.

The dream had been shattered that day on the football pitch at Richill - forever. Or had it?

Joe still had a burning passion for the game of soccer. He wasn't going to say good-bye to it that quickly. He might not be able to play but perhaps he could help others to play better. It wasn't too long till an opportunity came his way to fulfil this new ambition. Joe Peden was to become a kind of trainer- manager.

Over in the little village of Gilford, not far from where Joe lived, they had a football team - "Gilford United." Joe put the lads through their paces, toughened them up, taught them some of the team tactics he had learned as a player and did what he could to mould them into a more competitive force. But there was a more sinister aspect to the job, sinister that is in that it brought Joe face to face with temptation as he had never encountered it before.

A playing team had to be picked every week for the Saturday match and, of course, the boys had to meet in some convenient place to deliberate over such matters. The place they chose was the lounge bar of the local pub. It began with a meeting every Wednesday night but it wasn't long until they were meeting more and more frequently in the pub. Thursday night was added, then Saturday. Soon it became almost every night, except Sunday. The downward slide was gathering momentum.

5

THE DEMON DRINK

"My drinking habit started when I met with boys in the pub and had a few shandies. That's a mixture of beer and lemonade. But it wasn't long till I was drinking straight beer."

The Pedens moved house, to Banbridge and Joe got involved in the local team there - *"Banbridge Town."* But that led to further drinking problems.

The Banbridge team had a social club. Alcohol was now even more readily available. And when you've a liking for drink and it's available in quantity at cheaper prices, with less restrictions on closing times, you make the best of it. Joe did just that and the slide into the life of a drunkard was inevitable.

"When I got involved with the social club in Banbridge I sat down many an evening with a ten glass bottle of strong, dark rum and drunk the whole lot myself. Now you can imagine how I felt next morning after that!"

THE BROAD ROAD

When a man wants to go down the hill into a life of sin and foolishness, he'll find there's plenty of help. John Bunyan, in his *"Pilgrim's Progress,"* paints the picture well.

The broad road takes the weary traveller right past Vanity Fair, and in Vanity Fair, there's every worldly provision a man could desire.

If he wants to be entertained by lewdness and impurity - it's there. If dancing is his inclination - he can dance the night away until he has no feet left for it. If he'd rather sit with the boys and engage in foolish and filthy conversation - he'll have no want of companions. And if he prefers to drink himself senseless, night after night, in Vanity Fair he'll find ample provision for the slaking of his uncontrolled thirst. Yes, he can stroll through the avenues of Vanity Fair and pick whatever forbidden fruits of passion and desire satisfy his unregenerate heart. And all the while his godless companions will make the eating of those fruits easy for, "Fools make a mock at sin."

Joe Peden discovered there was all the help he needed to continue on his downward path. He was invited to take part in darts throwing, a big feature of pub life. As his talent developed he became a member of the pub's darts team. That, in turn, meant going around all the pubs in the district to play in the inter pub matches - and even more opportunities for drinking.

Inevitably, the drink became a real problem for Joe. He was no longer a *"social drinker,"* if there is such a thing. Instead of him taking drink - drink was taking him and he was powerless in its clutches.

EMPTY PROMISES

At this stage Joe still didn't realise the magnitude of his problem. Night after night as he left the house en route, yet again, for the pub, he gave Phyllis, his wife, a solemn promise that he would be home by a certain time. Of course, he never was.

"Very often a few of us got together in the social club for a card school, usually a few hands of poker. I was always one of the first people asked to join in and I was always keen."

"A card school was always an excuse to stay late at the club. We had the keys of the club and when everybody else had gone home we used to lock the doors from the inside and settle down for the night. Before you knew where you were the early light of dawn was tapping at the window."

Many a time Joe didn't come home all night. In the early hours of the morning he slipped into the house, changed his clothes and went straight back out again to work. And burning the candle at both ends, like that, made it very difficult to do a decent days work.

WARNING SIGNS

Looking back now Joe can see that the tell tale early signs of alcoholism should have been transparently apparent to him. But, at the time, he was totally blind to them.

"I suppose when the boss came to me at half past eight in the morning and told me to go out to the car, where there were a few bottles of beer, and to have a drink to help steady me up. I suppose when that happened I should have known there was something wrong."

Drinking to the extent that Joe was *"knocking it back,"* demands a lot of money. Good friend and all as the publican is, he doesn't provide too much drink if there's nothing to pay for it with.

"If I didn't pay for it, somebody else did. Most of the time it was my wife and children who paid for it. And again, that should have told me that there was something wrong with me. When you start going to clean your wife's purse out, or you break into the children's money boxes to get money for drink, you've got a serious problem."

However, throughout all this period very few people realised that Joe Peden was, in fact, an alcoholic. He displayed that same pleasing personality. He held down a good job as a foreman welder. He never missed church on a Sunday morning. Nobody knew the dark secret of his bondage to alcohol. Nobody that is, except his longsuffering, devoted and anxious wife.

"When I got drink I changed into a different creature. I was just like a Jekyll and Hyde. At first the drink made me happy and I started to sing. But then, as I got a taste more, I became the nastiest, most obnoxious person you could have met. At this stage I wanted to fight and as they say, *'If you'd looked at me sideways,'* I'd have drawn out and clouted you. Many a time my drinking sessions did end in a fight. It's to my shame I have to say that. That's the power of drink."

BAD INFLUENCE

One of the most perplexing of all the stories Joe can recall concerns his son Mark, then just ten years old. Mark loved the football too and asked his dad to take him along to watch the lads training. Joe relented and Phyllis agreed. "But bring him home at a reasonable time," she begged. But again, her words fell on seemingly deaf ears.

"I can see a wee lad of ten sitting beside me in the social club at half past two in the morning, crying and pleading *'Daddy will you not bring me home?'*"

The effect on Joe's wife was not unexpected. She took him aside, time and time again, in an effort to reform him. Sometimes she tried the gentle approach, appealing to his better nature, hoping his love for her and the children would result in sweet reason. At other times, in her frustration, she spoke more sharply, threatening to leave him and take the children with her. She even sought medical advice, in part for Joe, but mainly for herself, so great was the strain upon her.

Phyllis Peden is a very private person, not the kind of woman to go crying to others when life's knocks are suffered. She was just the same then. She never disclosed to anyone, not even the closest member of her family, her mother, what she was going through with Joe.

HEARTACHE

Night after night she sat by the bedroom window, watching and waiting for Joe to come home. She never knew how, or if he would turn up. Of course, he always did, somehow or other and usually he was drunk. Then it was her grim duty to cajole him into bed and to wake him next morning in time for work. Her vigilance cost her endless nights of sleep and took its toll on her own health.

There were constant visits to the doctor, endless remedies, an almost perpetual depression of spirit and more than once, near total mental breakdown. The strain of coping with a husband who was a slave to drink was almost unbearable.

Other people did notice that something was wrong. They noticed the pained expression and the drawn features on her once happy face. The listlessness, the depression and the constant strain were impossible to hide. But when enquiries were made Phyllis always had a plausible excuse for the way she looked and felt. Never once did she *tell tales* on Joe.

Eventually, of course the truth did leak out. Joe began to arrive home later and later. Phyllis had to send out search parties to look for him. No matter how discrete friends and family were asked to be, the word got around that Joe Peden was behaving badly. It wasn't too long after that till both Phyllis' mother and Joe's mother knew just what kind of a life Joe was leading.

The sad fact is that, throughout all this period of distress caused to Phyllis, Joe knew exactly what he was doing to her. He was sympathetic about her sickness and did his best to comfort her. But he didn't do the one thing that was most essential to help her. He didn't stop drinking. When the call of the pub came into his heart, he was off without another thought for his wife.

DRINKING!

"I knew what I was doing. I knew what was happening. Deep down inside I still had a love for my family. But when you're a drinking man you have to drink. Everything else, including the family, takes second place."

The only mitigating factor in the whole sorry saga is that neither Joe's wife or family ever suffered financial hardship. Joe was a good earner with a healthy wage packet at the end of the week. Even after he had given his wife what she needed to run the house, there was still a fair amount left for his own pocket. He also seemed to have enough sense to make sure that the necessary bills were paid before he went in search of pleasure. So the family was always well housed, well clothed and well fed. Materially, they wanted for nothing.

On reflection Joe would even admit that perhaps the fact that he was so well paid contributed to his downfall. Drink wasn't all that expensive and he had plenty of money for it.

However, it was the awful way that drink changed Joe that had the devastating effect on Phyllis.

It broke her heart to see her husband transformed, for the worse, by its power. Joe was normally a kind hearted, patient, considerate man. The kind of man who'd be first to help his neighbour in trouble. But when he took drink he was a different man entirely. He became nasty, aggressive, abusive and foul tongued. So much so that his wife and children had genuine cause to fear him.

All the efforts of wife and family to reform him were useless. Joe didn't need reformation, he needed regeneration and that was still a long way off. As was the case with the prodigal son in the gospels, Joe Peden would have to come to the place where he fain would have eaten the husks fed to the swine, before any change could begin.

Thank God, on that Saturday morning in 1975, Joe came to that place of hopelessness and help-lessness before God. All the crutches of the world, hitherto depended on, were taken away and he was left a spiritual cripple. Now and only now, in this stricken, smitten state, could God do something with him.

SALVATION!

The Rev. Frank McClelland was the minister of the Free Presbyterian Church in Tandragee. At his home that Saturday morning Joe was given a strong handshake and a warm welcome. Mr. McClelland ushered Joe into his study and sat him down. Before Joe could even begin to tell his story he broke down and started to weep openly and uncontrolably.

Through his tears Joe did his best to tell the minister just what kind of life he had been leading. He told him about the amounts of drink he was consuming. He confessed that his thirst for drink was so great that the children's money boxes were rifled to pay for his habit. He admitted that drink was destroying his life, his home and his family, and yet he was powerless to deliver himself.

Mr. McClelland listened patiently for a while as Joe continued his tale of disaster. Then he opened the Bible and began to read. He showed Joe that, despite all he had done, there was someone who loved him. He showed him, too, that the one who loved him could also deliver him from his strong master.

Opening the Bible at Isaiah chapter fifty three, Mr. McClelland preached Joe a short but telling sermon.

"All we like sheep have gone astray," he read.

Across the way in a field near the house a flock of sheep was quietly grazing. It gave the minister a natural opening for what he wanted to say. The illustration was simple, yet powerful. Sheep are timid creatures. But they're also foolish. No matter how well they're provided for they always seem to think that the grass on the other side of the fence is greener and sweeter.

STRANGE PASTURES

And we are so like sheep! We, too, have gone astray from God's perfect way. We have gone searching for strange pastures that look greener, but when we find them they don't satisfy. In fact the very opposite is the case. They disappoint us. Mr. McClelland read on.

"We have turned every one to his own way."

Sheep always want to go their own way. If there's a way out of the field at all, they'll find it, and be out through it in a moment. The trouble is they keep on wandering, farther and farther from the safety of their home pasture. And we're just the same. We insist on going our own way. We ignore God's way. And it's spiritual suicide.

In that brief sermon Joe learned just how foolish he had been. He had wandered far from God's way. He had broken through the fences of God's protection. He had strayed to the the strange pastures of worldly pleasure - and they did nothing for him. He had made a real mess of his own life and was making a pretty good job of messing up the lives of his wife and family too. But at last he was beginning to see the hopelessness of his position.

At this point the preacher tried to pour on some oil of healing. He turned to the best known verse in the Bible, John 3 verse 16; and read.

"For God so loved the world that he gave his only begotten Son, that whosoever believeth in him should not perish but have everlasting life."

"No matter how wicked a man has been, God still loves him," the minister continued. "And no matter how hopeless your case seems, God can still help you."

Joe was still unconvinced. He was so burdened and overpowered by the weight of his sin that he couldn't see any way of deliverance or escape. Satan had succeeded in leading Joe astray and now he was intent on blinding his eyes to the hope of the gospel.

"Do you believe the Bible is the Word of God?" Mr. McClelland asked Joe. Of course Joe had to answer that he did.

DOES GOD TELL LIES?

"Does God tell lies?" Again the minister waited for a response. He didn't have to wait long. Joe believed in God. He believed in the living and true God. He believed in a God who did not tell lies.

Mr. McClelland then turned in his Bible to Romans chapter 10, verse 13, and read:

"Whosoever shall call upon the name of the Lord shall be saved!"

Here was a promise from the God who does not tell lies. There were no conditions attached to it. Joe didn't have to do anything but call. But if he called, God would most certainly answer - and save him. Save him from the power of his sin, from the penalty of his sin, and even from the presence of his sin. It was just a plain, simple promise of deliverance and salvation. Would Joe accept it?

That final gospel arrow found it's mark in Joe's heart. The Holy Spirit applied the truth of God's word so convincingly that Joe was glad to call. Together, he and Mr. McClelland knelt to pray. Mr. McClelland committed the whole desperate case, and Joe, to the God of Heaven. Falteringly, but trustfully, Joe called upon God for his mercy and salvation.

"Lord, I'm just a sinner," he began. "But I believe you can save me from my sin. I believe that Jesus died upon the cross and shed his blood to deliver sinners like me. I ask you now to break the power of sin in my life, to deliver me from the chains that bind me and to make me a new creature. And I ask this all in the name of the Lord Jesus Christ."

When Joe got up off his knees he was a changed man. Indeed, he was transformed. A great burden rolled from his life and already the assurance of God's salvation filled his heart. He felt just like the central character in John Bunyan's classic story, "The Pilgrim's Progress." Pilgrim, when he stood at the cross and experienced deliverance from sin, cried out,

"Blessed cross, blessed sepulchre, yea blessed rather be, the man that there was put to death for me."

6

TELLING OTHERS

"Make sure you tell others what the Lord has done for you today. Bear witness of him to your family, your workmates and anybody else you come into contact with. If you stand up for Jesus, he'll bless you and look after you."

Those were the final words of advice offered by the Rev. McClelland as Joe Peden left the manse that Saturday morning in 1975, a new man.

Joe immediately drove over to see his mother and tell her the good news. Now Charlotte Peden wasn't a christian herself, but she wept at the news.

"You'll never regret it Joe," she said, and wished him all the very best. Already, the work of grace, wrought a short time ago in Joe's life, was bringing happiness to others.

From his mother's house Joe drove home as quickly as possible to tell Phyllis, his wife. Joe's behaviour in the past months and years had brought her nothing but misery and heartache. Obviously she'd be overjoyed to hear that Joe was saying good-bye to his old life. However, her reaction was far from what you might expect.

Joe remembers going in through the back door. Phyllis was standing at the sink washing dishes. He stopped beside her, put his arm around her, and said, "Phyllis, I've got saved this morning."

Phyllis never took her hands out of the sink but, continuing with the dish washing, turned to Joe and replied, "Well, we'll see how it goes."

SHOCK!

Joe was quite taken aback by this reaction. He fully expected Phyllis to be as excited as he was. However, with the benefit of hindsight he realises that his wife's attitude wasn't all that surprising. After all, how many times in the past had Joe come home, or been brought home in the stupors of drink and promised never to touch the stuff again? He had made a hundred solemn vows and broken them every one. To Phyllis, a promise from Joe was absolutely worthless. So why should this news make any difference to them?

Now it might seem that God gave Joe a rather tough start to his christian life. It could be suggested that things should have been a bit easier initially. Surely it wouldn't have been difficult for God to have made Phyllis Peden slightly more enthusiastic at the news of her husband's conversion. After all, her attitude could well have reacted adversely on Joe and made him think, "What's the use?"

However, it didn't, and Joe began learning some of the most important lessons of the christian life, very early.

First, the Bible says that men reap what they sow. That's one of God's basic laws. Second, God doesn't change His laws or allow people to circumvent them, just to make life easier. Just as sure as there's a sowing time, there's also a reaping time. It's true in the natural world - and it's equally true in the supernatural world.

Now Joe had been sowing bad seed for a long time. He had to expect a bad harvest, a harvest of distress, of shame and of distrust in him. It was unrealistic, even impossible, for the distrust of years to be erased in a moment, at the announcement of his conversion.

NEW FRUIT

The gospel produces fruit but it takes time for that fruit to mature. It's only when the fruit is mature that others will be impressed by the work of grace wrought in any human heart.

James, in his epistle, tells us that, "Faith without works is dead." Faith comes first, the works follow but it takes time for the works to be seen. In Joe's case it would take a very long time for his wife to be convinced that he was, indeed, a changed man.

But what about the effect on Joe. He could have been discouraged by his wife's reaction and given up, almost at the starting gate. Ah, but we must never loose sight of the grace of God in a man's conversion. This initial disappointment for Joe was the very first test of what had really happened that morning.

If Joe Peden was really saved, then nothing would deter him from following Jesus. If he wasn't saved then, perhaps, this was the best time to find out. Thank God, what took place that day has stood, and withstood, the test of time.

THE NEWS SPREADS

The news of Joe's conversion spread like wildfire. It wasn't very long till his brothers and sisters heard about it too. Christianity wasn't very strong in the Peden's, the only other believer was Jim, but they were a close knit family. For example, when trouble came to any member the others would normally rally round and lend a hand. So I suppose it's not surprising that a few of them came to the house that night.

Whether it was genuine interest or just plain old fashioned curiosity, Joe's not sure. Anyway they came. At first they were very quiet. The atmosphere was difficult, especially for them. They didn't really know what to say. It's kind of embarrassing to have to talk to your wayward brother about a sudden, radical change in his life.

And all the more so if you're ignorant of the grace of God yourself. I mean, just what do you say?

And so they sat, in whispered silence, looking back and forth at each other, being very pleasant, wishing, perhaps, it was time to go home. Supper was served. That broke the ice a bit. At least they could steer away from the possibility of having to talk about spiritual matters and make, instead, pleasant comments about the food.

Eventually people began to circulate a bit more. The serving of supper gave some an excuse to go into the kitchen, if only to help with the washing up.

One of Joe's brothers managed to get himself, as he thought, out of earshot and the question he put to Phyllis stands out to this day in Joe's memory.

"What happened to him?" enquired the brother who was completely mystified by the news. There was more than a hint of mystery in the reply that Phyllis gave him.

"I don't know. It was his own decision. Things just haven't been right for him!"

The entire conversation that night was about Joe's conversion. Politics was forgotten. Football, one of Joe's passionate interests, wasn't given a mention. And the television set wasn't even turned on. It was the first time in Joe's memory that "Match of the Day" wasn't watched on a Saturday night. It was also the first Saturday night in years that Joe hadn't been out drinking -

and hadn't been brought home drunk. What a change was already evident in his life!

Furthermore, up until that Saturday morning Joe had smoked, on average, a hundred cigarettes a day. From the moment of his conversion the desire for them had gone. It has never returned.

A NEW CREATURE

After the visiting members of family had gone, Joe and Phyllis sat for quite some time going over the events of the day. Once more Joe rehearsed his account of the visit to Rev. McClelland's home. He explained again, as best he could, how Mr. McClelland had shown him the way of salvation. He did his best to describe the simplicity of the moment when he knelt in prayer and sought God's mercy, and the sheer joy that flooded his heart when his burden of sin had rolled away.

Phyllis was still a bit apprehensive and sought assurance from Joe that this wasn't just a "flash in the pan". It would take some time to finally convince her that when God does a work in a man's life, it's a complete work. However, her husband came to bed that Saturday night sober - the first time he had done so for years.

One of the first decisions Joe had to make was which church he should attend. It wasn't a difficult decision really. Up till now church hadn't meant much to him. His interest in spiritual matters was non existent and he attended more or less out of habit. The Rev. McClelland had invited him to come along to his church any time, if he felt he would like to, so he decided to give it a try.

He went the very next morning, Sunday, and was astounded at the atmosphere in the place and the welcome he got. The gospels tell us," there is joy in the presence of the angels in Heaven when one sinner repents." Well, there was a lot of joy in Tandragee that week-end too, and a lot of people came to shake Joe's hand and tell him so. How they knew about him he has no idea, even to this day, but obviously the news had travelled fast.

When the organ introduced the first hymn and the congregation rose to sing, Joe was astounded. He had never heard such singing. It was full voiced, enthusiastic and sincere. And from the very first line the words seemed to have been written for him.

> *"It was down at the feet of Jesus,*
> *Oh that happy, happy day,*
> *That my soul found peace in believing*
> *And my sins were washed away."*

Joe was thrilled at the sound and the song. He'd never heard anything like this before. If this was God's salvation why hadn't he come to know it years before? It was heaven on earth!

FACING THE WORLD

Monday morning meant work of course. Joe was a welder and at times his work took him to various building and construction sites around the country.

In the same firm there was a lorry driver who delivered raw materials around the sites. He and Joe were what you might call, "good mates." They never socialised together but over the years they had built up a kind of a custom of meeting every Monday at lunch time to discuss the week-end just past.

As that first Monday lunch time of his christian life drew near, Joe wondered what kind of reaction there would be to the news he had to announce.

"Well Joe, what sort of a week-end did you have." The conversation was going, so far, just as Joe had expected. Obviously the news hadn't travelled into this man's circle of friends. Boy was he in for some surprise!

"I've got saved!" Joe told him, just as bluntly as that and then he explained the events of the previous Friday night and Saturday morning. Joe half expected either a tirade of abuse - or mocking laughter. But neither came. After the initial shock his mate just said, "Well Joe, it's the best life if you can keep it."

Right away the other work-mates saw a change in Joe. They remembered the times in the past when Joe had to be brought down off the scaffolding on a Saturday morning because he was suffering the after effects of a Friday night's drinking.

But the general reaction of his workmates surprised Joe. Again, he expected them to mock him, to re-christen him, "Holy Joe," (the temptation must have been great,) or to face him with outright opposition. However, none of these things happened.

Of course there were some who said, "I'll give you a week - or two weeks." But, in the main, there was great respect shown to him. Indeed, as time progressed, some of them raised the subject of salvation at times and asked Joe more about it.

8

A CHRISTIAN HOME

Since her own conversion Phyllis Peden has been a tremendous influence on Joe. She has supported and encouraged him and watching, with gratitude, his development as a gospel singer and preacher.

"If there's meetings to attend Phyllis is always the one to remind me of them and to make sure that I give enough time to prayer and preparation for them. She doesn't let me miss the prayer meeting either, no matter how tired I am when I come in after a day's work."

"She'll say, 'Remember what the Lord has brought you from Joe. I don't want you going back to what you used to be. I don't want you to backslide.'"

And yet, it was more than two years after Joe's life had been changed before Phyllis Peden's conversion took place. In fact it was so long after Joe's own experience that, when it happened, it took him almost by surprise.

OPINIONS

Even today Joe Peden's not the sort of man to force his opinions or ideas on anyone. He's rather meek and mild in his approach to people. Definitely not the sort of man to walk up to you in the street, thrust a gospel tract into your hand and tell you you're going to Hell unless you get saved. At the same time he's not a bit backward about declaring his faith in Christ. His singing and preaching ministry all across the country mean that he's well known for standing up for Jesus.

So when it came to the matter of his wife's conversion it seems that Joe adopted the right attitude, from the beginning.

Each Sunday morning Phyllis went to the church they had always gone to. Joe went to his new spiritual home, the Free Presbyterian church in Tandragee. He never objected to his wife going to her own church, or suggested that the one he went to was better. He never criticised her church, or its minister, in any way. That, he believed, was not the way to win his wife to the Saviour.

"Never, never did I attempt to say anything about the church or about the minister. I didn't then. I wouldn't now. The important thing was to live the Christian life in front of her and the Lord would do the rest."

"I believe that's also how I get on so well with people today too. I work with protestants and Roman Catholics. I work with people of all denominations and if I get an opportunity to witness to them I just present the gospel and leave the churches out of it. I've no time for running down other people or their religion."

SOFTLY, SOFTLY

Even though he felt that there was little or no chance of Phyllis coming into a personal relationship with Christ through the ministry of the man who occupied the pulpit in her church, finding fault with him was not the way to get her along to the gospel services in his own church. All that would do would be to make her dig her heels in further, to resist every invitation to hear the gospel in its fulness.

So Joe adopted the softly, softly approach. He lived a good christian life before her and the children. He let her see how the Lord had changed him. He was a living example of Paul's words, "If any man be in Christ, he is a new creature."

"She didn't see me just as a church goer. She began to see me as a man who was really saved."

As well as that, without realising it, he adopted the exact same tactics that his neighbour, Sammy Dunlop, had adopted when he was burdened for Joe. He prayed!

"Salvation is of the Lord," the Bible says and it's best left to the Lord. Sinners are never made to see the folly of sin and the dangers of Hell by cajoling, threatening or persistent badgering.

75

Conviction of sin, repentance and faith are all wrought in the hearts of men and women by the power of the Holy Spirit. Man's work is to witness by word of mouth, to win by example, and to pray.

"Through the Sunday sermons and the weekly Bible studies I was taught that God answered prayer. I was reminded very often that that's how I had come to the Lord - others had prayed for me. So I was encouraged by others to keep praying for my wife and that's what I did."

PRAYER

Every time he knelt down before the Lord in his private prayers he sought the Lord for the salvation of his wife. He asked the minister and members of the church to pray too and they did. Faithfully, week after week in the prayer meetings the name of Phyllis Peden was brought before the Lord in earnest prayer. And yet, for over two years nothing happened. At least, nothing outwardly visible happened.

The Rev. McClelland left Tandragee to take up duties as the first Free Presbyterian minister in Canada and still Phyllis wasn't saved. But his last words to Joe were "Don't be worrying Joe. Keep praying. Your wife will be saved!"

Still there were times when Joe wondered if that would ever be so. He longed for her to go along with him to the gospel meeting. He had learned that "Faith cometh by hearing and hearing by the Word of God." So it was important that she should be brought under the sound of the gospel. And yet he didn't feel that he should continually badger her to come with him on a Sunday evening.

What a delight it was then, and what a surprise when, on one Sunday night as Joe was getting ready for the gospel service, Phyllis announced "I think I'll go with you."

"I was over the moon," Joe recalls. "Then in the next breath she added 'Now don't be pestering me to go here every week.' So I didn't. She seemed to have made the decision to come when she wanted to and I just left it at that."

EXPERIENCE

That's an approach that might be unpopular with a lot of christians but it's one that Joe stands by and would advise. He quotes from experience.

"A fellow whose wife wasn't saved for over thirteen years adopted a completely different approach. He really did give his wife a difficult time of it by telling her that the Free Presbyterian church was the place she should be. He told her that she should be going there if she was going to be saved, in fact, he said she would never be saved anywhere else. But the outcome of that was that he completely turned his wife against the church and for years she wouldn't go near the place. In fact she hated it! Now she finally did get saved but it was nothing to do with his manner of witness to her."

Going back to his football days as a trainer/ manager Joe recalls the tactic he employed then for success.

"I got the best out of my players by having a good relationship with them. I used to coax them and bring them on in a gentle way. That got me results on the soccer field and I believe you can bring that same approach into the gospel. You can persuade people in a gentle way and consequently, you can win them."

DISCOURAGEMENT

However, there were times when he got discouraged too and wondered if she'd ever be saved. This was so particularly when Phyllis would say she was going along with him to the gospel meeting.

"I remember one Sunday afternoon she decided to go with me to hear Dr. Paisley. He was preaching in Lurgan and since Phyllis had never heard him she asked me to take her along to the service. I suppose there was a certain curiosity value about wanting to hear this much loved, much hated, much maligned and much misunderstood man."

Joe couldn't get Phyllis into the car quick enough and away they went, arriving in good time for good seats. Dr. Paisley preached a powerful gospel message and as always, there was an appeal at the end of the service to those who desired salvation.

Joe sat with his head bowed, quietly and earnestly calling upon the Lord to save his wife. Surely, after such a clear and dynamic message she must see her need of Christ if she was ever to have the hope of Heaven.

Surely there would be rejoicing in the Peden house this night, as well as in Heaven, over another sinner repenting.

The organ began playing softly and the congregation sang,

> *"Just as I am without one plea,*
> *But that thy blood was shed for me,*
> *And that Thou bidst me come to Thee,*
> *O Lamb of God, I come. I come."*

Again and again the verses were repeated. Again and again Dr. Paisley appealed to those who were not saved to raise a hand as an indication that they would like to come to know the Lord.

As the appeal continued, Joe prayed the more earnestly.

I thought to myself, 'It has to be today.'

However, Phyllis never budged. She seemed totally unmoved by what she had heard and came away from the meeting still unconverted. She left the meeting, apparently, as she had come.

As they got into the car and drove off towards home Phyllis turned to Joe and said "I suppose you thought my hand was going up in the air today. Did you?"

Joe replied that, indeed, he thought it would have.

"Well you've another think coming. It just didn't go up today. I knew all the time you were sitting there and you just thought I was getting saved today."

A LESSON

That experience was a real test to Joe's faith. He came home after that meeting with his spirits at a very, very low ebb. But it taught Joe a very valuable lesson. Joe Peden's time for his wife's conversion wasn't God's time and Joe had to learn that. However, his patience and prayerfulness eventually paid off and it was a time when he least expected it that he had the great joy of seeing his wife come to the Lord.

"She decided to come with me on another Sunday night to the gospel service. "A man called Trevor Gracey was the preacher that day and there had been five people saved at the morning service. During the meeting I noticed that Phyllis was a bit restless. However, when the sermon ended and the appeal was made for those who wanted to receive the Lord into their hearts, she never stirred. The last hymn was sung, the benediction was pronounced and the congregation began to file out of the building. We were actually going down the steps towards the car park when suddenly she bowed her head and began to weep."

"So I asked what the matter was and she said 'I would like to go back inside again.' What a joy it was for me to kneel with her in prayer and hear her call upon the Lord, as a humble sinner, for His salvation. It was a joyous occasion and I'll never forget it!"

"It just brought back to me the wonderful feeling of inner peace that I had experienced the day I was saved. I was flushed again with that joy of my first love for the Lord Jesus."

MOTHERS

There's little doubt that the power of mothers is vastly underestimated. In many ways the mother is the central figure in the home. She tends to spend much more time with the children. Consequently, she exerts a far greater influence on their character, their discipline, their values and their morals than many people, including mothers themselves, realise. That was no less true in the Peden household and the conversion of Phyllis made a tremendous difference in their home, immediately.

Over the two years since Joe's conversion he had never attempted to imposed his new christian values on the rest of his family. He believed them to be right and in keeping with the teachings of the Bible. He held them very strongly and he believed God would honour his obedience. However, he never thought it either wise or prudent to force his family, and especially his wife, to toe the new line. Much better, he thought, to adopt a more gentle, persuasive approach. That gentle, persuasive approach was seen in his manner around the house.

Before his conversion it was quite normal for the television to be on all day Sunday. But now that he was a christian he felt that Sunday was the Lord's day and should be spent differently. There were two church services to attend and very often an afternoon meeting somewhere too. The television programmes had a lot less attraction for him than hitherto.

But his family were still unregenerate. The glorious light of the gospel was, as yet, to shine into their hearts. They could not, with the Psalmist, proclaim "O taste and see that the Lord is good." In that condition what difference did it make whether they watched television on Sunday or Saturday?

TELEVISION!

And indeed, when you think about it, it's not so much when you watch television that matters, but what you watch. There are many christians who would probably have condemned Joe Peden for his attitude to his family's Sunday television habits. But many of the programmes they watch throughout the week are, to say the least, suspect.

One preacher, who used to work in the television business, once described the television set in terms of "an open sewer pipe, pouring all the filth and immorality of the world, into the home." That's not an unreasonable analogy. Just look at any of the "soaps" that so many people, including christians, are hooked on. Their entire philosophy is humanistic. God's name isn't held in reverence. God's laws aren't respected. God's ways aren't regarded. Success in the world is achieved by cheating, lying, backbiting, double-dealing and every other underhand method that can be summoned.

The tragic thing is that, when believers feed themselves on a weekly diet of such humanistic philosophy, they become tainted with the same set of values. Even more tragic is that those values filter through into the work and witness of the church.

Joe Peden's policy of not driving, but rather leading his family, by example, bore fruit. Even before his wife's conversion there was an acknowledgment that life for them would have to be different, now that the head of the house was a christian.

Phyllis was quick to realise and point out to Joe that the annual dinner dances, in connection with his work and the football scene, were no longer places to which he could go, without offending his conscience. His wife loved to dance, yet she gladly passed up those opportunities in favour of making life easier for her husband.

THE FAMILY ALTAR

When Phyllis became a christian there were even further changes and now they were made by mutual consent. Often they sat together, after that glorious day when Phyllis found the Lord, and discussed what they should do on many of these questions. Always, together, they sought to do what they believed was right in the eyes of God. It was a whole new experience for Joe.

"It was good that, once again, we could sit down together, as husband and wife, and discuss what we should do. It was really good that the partnership was there again and we were able to make the decisions together, before the Lord."

The home began to change right away, in the most wonderful way. One of the first and most significant things that happened was that Joe and Phyllis established a family altar in their home.

"We started to read the Bible together, something we had never done before. Phyllis used to ask me to read a passage of scripture and then explain it to her. After the reading we knelt together in prayer and asked the blessing of God upon our lives."

So the home of Joe and Phyllis Peden became what every home should be, a haven from the storms of life, a place of comfort and happiness, a Bethel, a gate of Heaven.

However, in later years, Joe's faith was to be tested again in the home. As his son Mark grew up into his teenage years, he began to share, less and less, his father's faith and principles. In fact, if the truth be spoken, he was openly rebellious to his father's position as head of the house. He used to complain openly to people about the strictness that Joe imposed and bemoan the fact that he couldn't do just as he pleased. In the eyes of his school-mates Joe Peden was painted as a real ogre, a killjoy, bent only on seeing that his rules were obeyed to the letter and with no concern for the happiness of his children.

Of course, that image was far from the truth. Yes, Joe did have a set of rules for his house and he insisted that they be obeyed. However, those rules were for the good of the whole house and Joe lived by them himself.

Joe was given grace to deal with the situation and in process of time Mark saw the sense of his father's discipline. Today, Mark is involved in the Lord's work himself and looking back, he often laughs about those days when he thought he was wiser and smarter than his dad. But then he's not the first young fellow to think that.

Today, all Joe's children are grown up, happily married and building homes of their own. What's more, they are each one following the faith of their father and mother. That brings Joe and Phyllis the greatest joy and contentment of all.

9

FIRST STEPS IN THE FAITH

"If you asked me if there was some part of my life I would not like to live again, it would be those years as a drunkard. It was absolute disaster."

Joe Peden talks very openly about those years of heavy drinking. He looks back on them with shame and, if the clock could be turned back, would love that those years could be erased. Nevertheless, God in his mercy has seen fit to use the lessons from Joe's experience to the blessing of others.

God is sovereign! He lifts up and He casts down. He builds and He destroys. He makes and He breaks.

In Joe Peden's case God allowed him to sink right down to the depths, to the place of agony, suffering and utter despair. Then, when he was at an end of himself, He lifted the helpless sinner up, set his feet upon the rock and transformed his life.

And yet Joe doesn't mind talking about what he once was.

"I think when you look back on those days it's a great reminder of what the Lord has delivered you from."

GREAT THINGS

Joe always uses one verse of scripture when speaking about himself. It's Psalm 126 verse 3. "The lord has done great things for us whereof we are glad."

He has no desire to glory in the events of his former life, but he just loves people to see what the Lord can do for a drunkard.

"I was a man who had wrecked his family life, broken his wife's heart and given his children nothing but unhappy memories. Surely the Lord has done great things for me. Do you not agree with me?"

Since then, Joe has given his testimony thousands of times, all over the country. His experiences have been a help and encouragement to multitudes.

"I've had letters and telephone calls from lots of people who have heard my testimony. Lots of wives, who have gone through exactly what my wife went through with me, have written to say how they've been encouraged by what the Lord did for me."

HONESTY

Joe believes it's important to be as open and honest as he is about his past, if he's going to keep on being successful at reaching people. There have been joyous occasions when people have been saved through Joe's testimony and very often what he has to say will challenge a husband who's going the same way as he went.

"Just a few weeks ago I got a phone call from a lady in Newtownards who had heard me giving my testimony on the radio. Her husband had lived a life very similar to mine and he had been saved just a few weeks earlier. But he was having a very rough time. I suppose the Devil wasn't giving up easily at the loss of one of his children and he was making life tough for this man. Anyway he heard me on the radio, was greatly encouraged and asked his wife to phone me and tell me so."

Joe can sit and repeat stories like those for hours on end. In the short sixteen years since he came to Christ he has built up a reputation as a likeable, friendly, quiet spoken servant of the Lord. A man who loves to sing the songs of Zion and who does it better than most. An able preacher of the gospel, and above all, a man of God.

DEDICATION.

It's probably true to say that the main reason for Joe's success has been his keeness, his dedicated approach to living the life of a christian, right from the word go.

When Joe Peden became a christian he went at his new faith just the way he went at his football - with everything he had.

There would be no second best for him. No playing on the sidelines and certainly no spectating from the grandstand. He would be in there giving it all he had.

"I realized right away that, if this change which had taken place in my life was to have any chance of developing, I would have to co-operate in that development. That meant attending the Sunday services. It meant being at the prayer meeting, and it meant getting involved in the young people's fellowship."

The Rev. Frank McClelland, who had shown Joe the way of salvation, had advised him to get involved as much as possible in God's work.

Joe had been very busy in the world. He'd had many interests. Now they were all gone - there would be a vacuum. That vacuum had to be filled with something. If it wasn't filled with service for God there was a great possibility that Joe could slip back into the world again.

A LESSON

One of the first lessons Joe learned, as a young, new born christian concerned his former love - football. Like many another person in the same situation Joe didn't give up his interest in football immediately. A passion like that doesn't always die overnight and he felt that to watch the odd match wouldn't do him any harm.

The week after he was saved Joe went to Shamrock Park, in Portadown, to watch the local team playing a side from Larne.

Now you must remember that he had never stood among the spectators before. He had always been on the playing field and a good distance from the crowd. So he wasn't really prepared for what was to come.

"Suddenly, half way through the match I became very aware of all this foul language which filled the air. As well as the usual oaths and curses and the abuse hurled at the players and the referee, there was a continuous blaspheming of the Lord's name. It was very offensive and very grievous and I'm sure it grieved the Lord too. I didn't want to be part of it and there and then made a vow that if the Lord took me out of there that day, I would never be back."

Well the Lord did take him out of Shamrock Park, but still his interest in football wasn't quite dead.

He thought about the possibility of managing a junior side. Perhaps he could even be of some christian influence on the young lads who came to play. In fact, during this time he was offered the running of the junior club in Banbridge. But he wasn't sure what to do.

ADVICE

He asked the Rev. McClelland for advice. Mr. McClelland couldn't, or perhaps wisely, wouldn't be specific. He wouldn't say either do or don't. But he did lay down some guidlines.

"I can't tell you what to do," he said. "But whatever you decide to do make sure it's what the Lord wants of you."

"But how can we know what the Lord's will is," Joe enquired.

"The Lord can speak in many ways," replied Mr. McClelland, "But very often it's through His Word. So read the Bible as much as you can. And pray! And when God shows you his will, you'll know."

Joe was being pressed by the old football pals to take up the duties as manager for the junior team. He asked the men for more time to think it over. He promised to come back to them with an answer within the week. He realised he would have to be even more earnest in his quest for an answer from the Lord.

GOD SPEAKS

Just around this time, in the weekly Bible class, they were studying the book of Isaiah. Joe was sitting at home one evening reading from Isaiah when suddenly a verse seemed to spring out of the page at him.

It was chapter forty three and verse eighteen.

"Remember ye not the former things and neither consider the things of old."

"Just like that, the Lord spoke to me and showed me that the football was a thing of the past and that I should forget all about it. I just said 'Lord that's it,' tore up all the forms and papers to do with the football club, put them in the fire and later, told the boys I wouldn't be near the football club."

"That was one of the greatest lessons I ever learned. Furthermore, as a young christian, it was a great thrill to me that the Lord had spoken to me through His Word."

However, there was one final lesson to be learned concerning the football and Joe's involvement in it.

STUNNED!

A short time after God had spoken so clearly from his Word, a few christian friends invited Joe to join them for a friendly match - just a bit of fun to while away an evening. The teams were made up lads from the local Free Presbyterian and Baptist churches, plus a few other christians from other places. A former Linfield player, now well known evangelist, Billy Kennedy, was there too.

During that game, quite accidentally but dramatically as it turned out for Joe, one of the young players sustained a broken leg. As the crowd of players, including Joe, gathered around him to lend assistance, Joe was almost stunned by the voice of God. Here was he, Joe Peden, former footballer, instructed by God to "remember not the former things," once again witnessing an accident on the football field.

It was enough. From that moment Joe ceased to have any affiliation with, or interest in football. He has never been to a football match since. He doesn't even watch the F.A. Cup Final on televsion.

However, that was Joe Peden's decision regarding his personal involvement in football. He'd be the last man to legislate a similar position for every other christian.

CHRISTIANS IN SPORT!

Many christians today argue that they can involve themselves in sport, in public life and even in the entertainment world. They maintain that it's better for them to be amongst the young as an example than for the ungodly to exert their influence.

When faced with this question Joe Peden has a stock answer.

"What I decided before God was for Joe Peden. The football wasn't for me. All the things associated with football, the social clubs, the drinking and so on, were the things that brought about my downfall. If I had stayed amongst those associations they would have assured my downfall again."

"But there's something else you have to remember. Football today enjoys a lot of sponsorship from drink companies. They put up the money and thus make possible a lot of the sporting activities that young people get involved in. Now I don't think it's right for anyone to be involved in something sponsored by a booze company. Especially so, if they have to wear a jersey with a brewers name splashed across it. I don't think that honours God, in any way."

As well as that Joe believes it's much easier for a christian to be pulled down by the influence of the majority in sport, than for one christian to pull the others up. There are too many temptations, too many opportunities for wrong things to be either said or done, to make it a wise proposition for any christian.

THE CHILDREN

During all this time, unknown to Joe, the Rev. McClelland had been praying for someone to take up the burden of starting a children's work in Tandragee church. He had approached a number of people about it but no one had taken up the challenge. In due course he left for his new ministry in Canada without seeing his vision realised.

Shortly after Joe's decision to make his break with football he was out with Isaac Hazely and the rest of the team in the open air witness. They used to go around different housing estates, in the summer evenings, singing and preaching the gospel.

It was a great way to loose your fear of what people thought of you and to strengthen your courage for the Lord. It was also the place where many young christians cut their teeth in service and in testimony for Christ. A great proving ground.

On one of these nights a crowd of children gathered around the meeting and since Joe was always very fond of children, he went in among them and began to chat to them. Eventually, he asked if they'd like someone to come around the estates and hold a few children's meetings. The children were delighted with the idea and so the idea of a children's outreach was born.

It wasn't long after that till a few of them put their heads together and decided to do something positive about it. They approached the church elders, outlined their plan and received their immediate blessing on it. Joe Peden became the leader.

The children's work grew apace. Within a very short time as many as a hundred and seventy children were coming to the church every week for the children's meetings. As well as that the children's workers carried through their first intention of going around the housing estates in the area to hold open air meetings, specially for boys and girls.

God blessed their efforts and many, many children were brought to know Christ through their efforts. Many of them went on to grow up in the church and in turn, to play their part in further outreach.

GOD'S PURPOSE

It was mainly through his involvement in the work amongst the boys and girls that Joe began to first see that God had a greater purpose in saving him than just the deliverance from eternal doom. God doesn't just save them to give them some kind of spiritual "fire insurance policy." There's much more to it than that. God saves men to serve Him. And in going out into the surrounding area to reach the children for Jesus, Joe was obeying the injunction of the Master, "Son, go work today in my vineyard," and "Go ye into all the world and preach the gospel to every creature."

Yes, God had saved Joe Peden for a purpose. The first time that the Rev. Frank McClelland returned from Canada to visit Northern Ireland, and Tandragee in particular, he had something very special to say to Joe about that purpose for his life.

"You don't realise the thrill that I got when I heard there was a children's work in Tandragee." And then he added, "Did you ever stop to think that God saved Joe Peden, a man who was a drunkard, so he could start a children's work in

Tandragee? Always let that be an encouragement to you Joe."

In course of time, when the demands of other ministries made greater claims on his time, Joe had to hand over the reins of the children's work to new leaders. However, the ministry among the boys and girls, which he started in such a small way, continues and prospers. Indeed, only eternity will reveal what has been achieved by the service and dedication of Joe Peden to others and to his Lord.

10

EARLY INFLUENCES

An old christian gentleman was once giving his testimony and in a rather boastful way proclaimed that he had been, "forty years on the road to Heaven."

Under his breath, someone who knew him quite well muttered, "More like forty years in the road."

Sadly, that's the case with so many people who have known the Lord for a long time. It's equally true of a lot of people who know him only a short time too.

A lot of young christians face more early discouragement, not from the world, but from those who profess the name of Jesus. Indeed, it's a wonder that so many of those who come to the Lord ever get beyond the cradle stage, such is the attitude of others in the faith.

The book of Revelation speaks of the zeal of the believer's first love for the Lord. And it has to be seen to be believed. What a wonderful thing it is to see new born babes in Christ consumed with love for their Saviour. They will climb mountains, cross streams, face the heat of the desert and the fiercest opposition of Hell, to tell others of Jesus, the King of kings.

SACRIFICE

No burden is too great to bear. No task is too difficult. No price is too high to pay, that the name of Jesus be emblazoned on the heart of every human soul. With young believers, sacrifices are readily and willingly made.

If you want doors knocked and people invited to a gospel mission or a special service - ask young christians! If you want gospel tracts distributed in the busy shopping centre of downtown anywhere - ask young christians! If you want help with an open-air meeting in the middle of the roughest, toughest estate in the land - ask young christians. They're full of vitality, enthusiasm, interest, passion and raw zeal.

Oh, very often it needs to be tamed and tempered a bit - but just a bit. So often it's killed - suffocated and stifled before it ever gets a chance to develop.

Such was not the case, however, in the young christian life of Joe Peden. Right from the start he was well influenced and suitably encouraged.

ISAAC HAZELY

Isaac Hazely was no killjoy and not a man to restrain the exuberance of christian youth. On the contrary, he was a man who knew how to encourage, to assist and to hone to perfection those who were young in the faith. Like precious, uncut diamonds, he would take those who were young in the faith and by example and encouragement, work with them till they sparkled like jewels in the Master's crown.

Isaac was the man who ran the open-air meetings in Tandragee. He had been running them for twenty-five years. Long before there was ever a Free Presbyterian Church in Tandragee, Isaac Hazely and his little team stood at the top of the town on a Saturday night or a Sunday afternoon and proclaimed the old fashioned, simple gospel of salvation, by grace, through faith.

Isaac Hazely was a spark, an electrical contractor and long years before anybody else he had gadgets and devices to enable him to play gospel records through the loudspeakers. Week after week, faithfully throughout the years, the songs of the gospel would echo down the main street in Tandragee and passers by would be blessed by the sounds of "Amazing Grace," "The Old Rugged Cross," "The Ninety and Nine," "What a Friend we have in Jesus," and many others.

AT THE MICROPHONE

As soon as Joe Peden started coming to the church regularly Isaac took him under his wing. He was immediately invited to the open-air meeting at the top of the town and very soon was standing at the microphone giving his first faltering words of testimony. Isaac stood close behind him, ready to whisper a verse of scripture, if Joe got tongue tied or stuck. Joe showed potential and enthusiasm and that was enough for Isaac.

"Isaac was a tremendous encouragement to me in the early days. As well as the open-air opportunities he encouraged me in other ways too. The very first time I ever read the scriptures in public it was for Isaac Hazely, in the prayer meeting in Tandragee. I was shaking like a leaf that night but it was a marvellous experience. He encouraged me to pray in the meeting too."

The Rev. Frank McClelland was another one who gave Joe a lot of help in his early christian life. Very often he would come up to Joe, put his arm around him and whisper some words of encouragement.

"I remember one Sunday morning just after I was saved. I was coming out of the prayer meeting just before the start of the morning service and Frank called me aside and said 'I want to speak to you for a moment, Joe.'"

"I thought to myself 'What's up here?' I though he was going to tell me to get my hair cut. It was still rather long. However, instead of that he put his arm around me and said 'I was talking to the Big Man,' that was Dr. Paisley 'and I was telling him all about you. He told me to tell you that they're praying for you and you're to keep looking to the Lord.'"

It may seem a very small thing to many people, but to Joe Peden, young in the faith and still finding his feet along the christian pathway, it was a spiritual tonic.

"On one occasion I was invited up to Sixmilecross to give my testimony. As soon as I arrived there the people informed me that Frank McClelland had told them all about me and had asked them to pray for me. And I was aware of the effect of those prayers. That's where the strength came from. That's why I was able to stand in the open-air and witness for the Lord."

"On another occasion Frank asked me to give my testimony in the church in Tandragee. I agreed to do it but I was so nervous on the night. My legs were like jelly, my knees were knocking and my whole body was trembling. The only thing that settled me down and enabled me to go on was Frank reminding me that a lot of people were praying for me."

THE FUNNY SIDE

Of course there were the humorous or the embarrassing moments too. One night, again at the open-air meeting with Isaac Hazely and friends Joe was asked to take part. By this time he had developed a bit of a talent for singing and that's what he agreed to do. A fair number of people had gathered around to listen as Joe stepped forward to the microphone and began to strum his guitar and sing.

"I was getting along just fine and enjoying spreading the good news of the gospel in song when, suddenly, half way through the piece I completely forgot the words. Nobody else standing about seemed to know the song so they couldn't help me. There was no Isaac to whisper them to me on this occasion. Anyway, only slightly daunted I had another go - from the beginning of the verse."

"The second time around the same thing happened. When I got to that certain line in the song everything went blank. I couldn't even make a stab at it. Eventually, I just had to give up and slink away to the back of the meeting, embarrassed and feeling rather sorry for myself. Suddenly from being on top of the world I was down in the valley of despair. But I got over it."

NOT SO FUNNY!

There were the less humorous episodes too. Like the time, again in the open-air, when a drunk man decided to test their metal by hurling abuse at them.

"It was in Poyntspass and this man came out of the pub very upset, very angry. He stood in the middle of the street and cursed and swore about God. The things he was saying actually frightened me."

'Who is God?' he called out.

'Where is God? If there really is a God in Heaven let Him strike me down dead now!'

"He made fun of the young people who were speaking and giving testimony too. Really, the whole thing was quite frightening."

"At this time the minister in Tandragee was the Rev. Harry Cairns and he took hold of the situation. He stepped forward to the microphone and uttered just one verse of scripture,

'The fool hath said in his heart, there is no God.'

"The effect of these words was like hitting the man with a whip. He went absolutely wild with rage and didn't like being called, even by implication, a fool."

"However, Mr. Cairns instructed the young people to continue with the meeting while he went and had a personal talk with the man. It didn't do very much good, however, and peace wasn't restored until some of the other people in the public house came and took the drunk man away."

"Thankfully, it did all end quite peacefully but it was very frightening at the time."

A WEE WORD!

All these situations and experiences were building up Joe's confidence as a singer and as a public speaker. In course of time he was invited to, as they say in christian circles "Bring a wee word."

"The first time I ever preached, if you could call it that, was at an old people's home in Portadown. I spoke for all of six minutes! That six minutes took about a two weeks to prepare but then I had no idea of how to go about such a task. I've learned a wee bit since then."

For someone like Joe, who had played before thousands of people in football cup finals, speaking in front of a handful of people should have been no trouble. However, it doesn't work like that.

"It was a horrifying experience. I didn't believe anyone could be so nervous. I must have drunk a gallon of water before it and another gallon after it was all over. It certainly was thirsty work."

TALENT SPOTTED!

In more recent times the present minister of Tandragee Free Presbyterian Church has been a great encouragement to Joe. He first met the Rev. Austin Allan about eight years ago and quickly became very friendly with him. No-one was more delighted than Joe when, about a year later,

Mr. Allan became the minister of the Tandragee church.

"I must pay special tribute to Mr. Allan. He has been a tremendous encouragement to me in my own singing and preaching ministry. He regularly asks me to stand in for him when he has to go and preach elsewhere. It's been my privilege to conduct both the prayer meetings and sometimes the Sunday services in his absence and I always enjoy that."

Until the Rev. Allan arrived in Tandragee Joe had never taken a meeting there. However, Mr. Allan very quickly recognised Joe's talent and set about making room for it. It was he who invited Joe to conduct special youth missions and children's services in Tandragee and has given him full support in doing that.

When Joe's mother and then Phyllis' mother both died within a short time of each other Mr. Allan was a tower of strength. He was there at the hospital and then in the home to provide support, encouragement and sympathy just when it was most needed.

He takes a great interest in Joe's ministry too. Joe is very often absent from the services in Tandragee by dint of the fact that he's all over the country himself ministering to others. Far from chiding Joe about this, as some men in the same position might be inclined to do, Mr. Allan encourages him and reminds the believers in Tandragee to keep Joe to the fore in their prayers.

"Joe's the kind of man who does whatever he's asked to do, willingly and well. He's very reliable, very dependable. He has a particular talent with young people and a very winning way with them. When it comes to the preaching of the Word he's absolutely faithful and yet, at the same time, extremely considerate of the feelings of people. His ministry has always been widely accepted and well commented upon in our church.

"But I like Joe as a friend too. We've had many good times of fellowship in the Lord's work and many good times just getting together socially."

Rev. Allan maintains a continuing interest in where Joe is preaching, who he is with and what success is attending his labours in the gospel. But then that's the kind of man Joe Peden is. He attracts friendship and respect wherever he goes.

11

A NEW SONG

Even before he was saved Joe Peden loved to sing. God had blessed him with a good voice and an ear that could hold a tune. Singing seemed to come naturally to him.

When the people he worked for had a Christmas dinner dance, or some other kind of a do, there was always a group there to provide the music. It was always the custom and still is, to ask a few people from the audience to come up and give the crowd a song or two. Joe's was always the first name down on the list and he was always happy to oblige.

He sang the country hits of the time, that was his favourite style and many an hour's entertainment he gave to the people on the dance floor with his renderings of "The Wild side of Life," and "Almost Persuaded," the country song that is, not the popular hymn.

He was an Elvis fan too and had bought a copy of the Presley version of "How Great Thou Art."

It did something for Joe, this rendering of the now very popular hymn. "Like shivers up and down my spine," he describes it. So it's not surprising that now and again "How Great Thou Art," was part of Joe's repertoire on these big nights.

As soon as he was saved Joe realised that singing was something that was very popular in christian circles too. His only talent, though, was singing. He couldn't play any musical instrument. But shortly after he got saved he bought himself a six string guitar.

"It was very cheap, it cost about £20 and I didn't even know how to tune it. But Isaac Hazely's daughter could play guitar so she showed me how to tune the thing. I must have been fairly hard to teach because Jill, Frank McClelland's daughter, gave me a few more lessons on tuning. Anyway, between the two of them they got me started."

PRACTICE MAKES PERFECT!

For weeks and months after this Joe would go into the bedroom in the evenings and practice the various chord sequences on his new guitar. Somebody has said that learning to play a musical instrument is one per cent inspiration and ninety nine per cent perspiration. Joe would agree with that. At the beginning a lot of the noises coming from the guitar were anything but attractive. There were the usual thumps and bangs and discordant sounds. But, with persistance, he acquired a bit of skill and could pick out and strum the right chord at the right time. He began to accompany himself as he sang. Eventually, he was asked to sing and play in public.

"I was asked to pick out one piece and come and sing it at a meeting in the old people's home. I remember well the piece I chose. It was a song written by Johnny Gimble and recorded by Merle Haggard and a good few other country singers."

'Guide me Lord, through the day.
Guide me Lord, this I pray.
Through all hardship, temptation and strife.
Guide me Lord, through the night.
Guide me Lord, by Thy light
That Thy will may be done in my life.'

After his initiation at the old people's home he was asked to sing at the Young People's Fellowship, in Tandragee and further invitations followed.

The Rev. Reggie Cranston heard Joe singing one night at a meeting Tandragee and invited him up to Omagh, to sing there. In Omagh someone else gave him a further invitation to sing somewhere else and so the singing ministry blossomed.

A WIDENING MINISTRY

All this time, of course, Joe was practising away and learning new songs, adding to his repertoire. He was developing his skills as a preacher too and the singing opened up a lot more doors to his ministry. In a very short time he was travelling the length and breadth of the country singing and preaching the gospel.

The guitar is still his favourite instrument, although there are still some people who frown upon its use in gospel circles. They suggest that it's an instrument that's been used and abused in worldly music and perhaps smacks too much of the world. However, surely it's only an instrument and because some people misuse it is not a justification for banning it.

There is nothing in this world that some men will not misuse. However, should that prevent the proper use of those things. Men misuse money but christians make good use of it to the extension of Christ's kingdom. Men misuse their God given talents to the ruination of their own souls and the souls of others. Christian's dedicate their talents to the service of Christ.

One of the things that men most misuse is their own bodies. They give them over to the service of self and the Devil, giving them over to sin and uncleanness of every kind. But as temples of the Holy Ghost what great use the saints down through the ages have made of them for the glory of God.

IN GOD'S HANDS!

A guitar is just something else that, in the right

hands, can be used to attract sinners to the gospel and win them for Christ. If God could use a rod in the hands of Aaron; or the jawbone of an ass in the hands of Samson; or a sling in the hands of David; surely he can use a guitar in the hands of Joe Peden.

What Aaron and Samson and David had in common was not the instruments they used, but their sanctified dedication to the God of Heaven. Joe Peden displays that same virtue of character.

Joe Peden favours the use of the guitar for his own personal musical ministry. Very often when he goes to meetings local organists aren't familiar with the songs he sings. They can't be expected to sight read them to accompany Joe. Furthermore, they're not familiar with his style and phrasing. If they do try, with their best efforts, to make an attempt at it, very often the result is more embarrassing than edifying. When Joe accompanies himself he can alter the pace and the style to suit the occasion and it makes for a much more relaxed performance.

GIVING GOD THE BEST!

Perhaps this is also in line with his whole thinking about his service for his Lord. He wants it to be the best, the very best that he can do. So often, so many christians seem to go about the Lord's work with a 'do rightly' attitude. But not Joe Peden. Even though people don't have to pay to hear him sing and preach he still gives them good value. Even though he's not singing professionally he still adopts a very professional approach to everything he does. There's no such thing as second best as far as he's concerned.

"I remembered what I had given to the world. I remembered with what zeal I had served the Devil and I felt the Lord couldn't be offered anything less. So that's why I felt I had to go at it with all my heart - and keep at it"

However, he's not above criticism. His wife, Phyllis, sees to that.

"My wife is my best critic. And she's very honest and open. If I don't preach well she tells me. If I don't sing well she also tells me. If there's something that needs to be improved Phyllis will tell me - and tell me very straight. I pay heed to that and make the necessary adjustments and that's the way we work together. Sometimes she would tell me that the guitar was a bit too loud so next time I know I have to stroke it that little bit softer. Or if I'm preaching in a small hall she will tell me I raised my voice a bit too much. Next time I'll keep that in mind."

In all this Joe realises that Phyllis has his interests at heart and he looks upon her constructive criticism as a great asset to his ministry. He's a fairly willing student, too. He likes to know how any part of his ministry can be improved and does his best to make the adjustments Phyllis suggests.

MUSICAL INFLUENCES

But of course his wife hasn't been his only influence. As soon as he began singing, indeed as a soon as he was saved, he started listening to the music of Rev. William McCrea. It wasn't long till he met him and immediately they became firm friends.

"In my opinion he was a tremendous gospel singer and I started to buy his albums right away. I took to the man and to his style of singing right away. But I never thought I'd ever have the privilege of sharing a platform with him."

However, he did and one night he found himself preparing to go along to Portadown to sing in the same meeting as Mr. McCrea.

"For the whole week before the meeting the thought was building up inside me that I was going to sing in the same meeting as the Rev. William McCrea. It was almost overpowering. But I remember Phyllis saying to me 'Look you're going to sing for the Lord so just go and sing.'

"But I just couldn't get over this feeling of nervousness. How could I sing in the presence of so great a gospel singer. In my mind I had him built up away out of all normal proportion.

"However, when I arrived at the meeting place one of the first people I met was Mr. McCrea. He immediately struck up a very warm and friendly conversation. This had a great settling and calming effect on me so that when it came my turn to sing I didn't feel so nervous after all."

NEW FRIENDSHIPS

At this point it has to be pointed out that the Rev. McCrea is not only a fine singer, he's also a very accomplished musician, playing either piano, organ or accordion. As soon as Joe began to sing Mr. McCrea joined in on the organ and provided a superb accompaniment. This gave Joe great encouragement.

After the meeting Mr. McCrea invited Joe to come to his church in Magherafelt to sing there and to give his testimony. Since then they've sung together in praise services all over the country and have become the best of friends.

"I rate him as a tremendous person. Not the man I had initially built him up to be but a humble, devoted servant of the Lord Jesus. He's been a great encouragement to me in my singing and given me a lot of help over the years. Even today, there's meetings I would go to and Mr. McCrea would request that I sing particular songs - something that I could never have imagined happening. Such is the nature of the man."

By the same token the Rev. William McCrea has nothing but the highest praise for Joe.

"Joe Peden is just a gracious, godly big fellow and a man I hold in the very highest esteem. It's my privilege to know him as a true friend. We've had many times of great fellowship together in the gospel and it's always Joe's desire to see precious souls come to know our Lord Jesus Christ. His singing is natural, down to earth and from the heart. He's just himself. He doesn't try to put on any airs and graces and I like him for that."

Joe Peden has never tried to model himself on anyone, not even the Rev. McCrea. He believes, both in the singing and the preaching, that he should be himself - that's the only way he can sure of God's blessing.

CRITICISM!

There are, sadly, some people who object to the type of music that Joe and Mr. McCrea sing. They say its country style is too much like the sort of thing that Joe would have sung in the pubs in his unconverted days. Joe is not particularly bothered by their criticisms.

"I'm not troubled about what other people may think about me or my music. I know what the Lord has delivered me from. I have no intention of going back to that old life. Deep down in my heart I know that what I'm doing is being done in all sincerity for the glory of the Lord. What other people think or say doesn't cause me to worry. Let's put it that way."

"I was born in sin and lost but Jesus paid the cost
To pardon me from all iniquity.
But till I see His face I really need His grace
To guide me o'er the paths He planned for me.

Guide me Lord, through the day.
Guide me Lord, this I pray.
Through all hardship, temptation and strife.
Guide me Lord, through the night.
Guide me Lord, by Thy light
That Thy will may be done in my life.'

God loves us everyone and gave His only Son.
To save our souls from sin He gladly died.
So trust in Him today, He'll wash your sins away
And daily He will be your light and guide."

Johnny Gimble

12

IT'S NOT AN EASY ROAD

It's a solemn but true fact that the road to Heaven is by no means an easy one. Jesus said "In the world ye shall have tribulation, but be of good cheer, I have overcome the world."

Only eternity will reveal what trials, sorrows and tribulations the saints of God have had to overcome on their earthly sojourn.

The Old Testament records how the children of Israel were made to wander in the wilderness for forty years to test them, to purge them and to prove them.

The New Testament saints were given no more different treatment. Paul's epistles abound with words of encouragement to those who are going through the vale of affliction.

Indeed such affliction, as we refer to it, is a hallmark of the Christian, an evidence that he does, in fact, belong to the Lord. "If ye be without chastisement, whereof all are partakers, then are ye bastards and not sons." A clear indication that

God disciplines his children with the rod of his correction.

The professing christian's response to such correction indicates his relationship with God. And that response measures the sincerity of his love for the Lord. "The Lord your God proveth you, to know whether ye love the Lord your God with all your heart and with all your soul." The true possessor of God's salvation will bow and yield to the correcting hand of God. The empty professor will rebel and complain. Someone has said that in times of correction true saints fly to the Lord, hypocrites fly at the Lord.

FAITH TESTED

However, as well as the chastening which every believer is subjected to from time to time there is the testing, or trying of faith. True faith will and must be tested!

A godly christian man and woman were suddenly plunged into the depths of grief when their son was killed in a tragic accident. As you can imagine they were broken and devastated by the event. The minister came to see them and almost the first words he spoke, after offering his heartfelt sympathy, were "If your faith cannot stand this test, then it is worthless." On the face of it those may seem un-sympathetic, almost harsh, words. However, when you think about them, they are absolutely true. If professed faith in

Christ is true faith - then it must stand the test of life.

Peter was inspired to write "Think it not strange concerning the fiery trial which is to try you, as though some strange thing happened unto you." And again he writes "The trial of your faith, being much more precious than of gold that perisheth, though it be tried with fire."

Joe Peden is no different to any other true Christian that has ever lived. He has known both the chastening of the Lord and the trial of faith in his life. That trial has been evidenced perhaps most of all in the ill health he has endured.

SICKNESS

Shortly after his conversion Joe was stricken with severe stomach pains. A hospital appointment was arranged and colitis, a complaint of the bowel, was diagnosed. It so happened that the hospital consultant was a saved man, a Mr. Mulligan and he immediately spotted the 'Jesus Saves' badge in the lapel of Joe's jacket. Right away a discussion on the things of God took place between them and Joe's past was brought out. Mr. Mulligan was able to explain that the abuse of alcohol was one of the biggest causes of the illness Joe was suffering from.

That, however, didn't make the problem go away. For eight long years Joe was on daily medication prescribed by the hospital. The fact that he was now a christian didn't remove the illness. However, now that he was a christian and no longer drinking to excess, a gradual healing took place and surgery, at one time contemplated, wasn't necessary. The Lord did give healing but a large part of it was through his delivering Joe from the power of strong drink.

Another thing his illness taught Joe was the importance of proper rest.

"There were times when I would have been in the best of health for eight or nine months at a time. At these times I was really busy in the Lord's work and being so zealous, I didn't know when to stop. Suddenly this trouble would flare up again and I would have to take things a lot easier, sometimes even stop for a while till I recovered. I believe that was the Lord's way of setting me aside for the rest I needed."

NONE INDISPENSABLE

Sometimes people who are in the Lord's work unconsciously adopt an attitude of indispensability. They seem to think they can't be done without. They've either forgotten, or never heard the little verse that goes,

> *"Take a bucket and fill it with water*
> *Put your hand in it up to the wrist.*
> *Pull it out and you'll find in a moment*
> *The measure of how you'll be missed.*

You may splash all about when you enter
And stir up the water galore
But stop, and you'll find in a moment
It seems just the same as before."

Joe Peden was working hard all day in his employment and then driving all over the country, night after night, to sing and preach.

The physical strain was immense, so setting him aside was another way of easing the burdens of ministry brought on by his ever increasing popularity.

He came home one night, very late, after having just driven from Limavady. Opening his diary he leafed through the pages and saw what was lined up for the next three weeks. There were meetings booked in churches and halls all across the country. The miles he would have to drive were staggering, to say the least. "How will I ever get through all this Lord?" he mused.

"About half past two in the morning I woke with this stabbing pain in my side. At half past nine that same morning I was in Craigavon hospital being prepared to be wheeled down to surgery for an appendicitis operation. The next three weeks that I was so worried about was completely wiped out.

"But at that time I was so physically exhausted I just didn't know how I was going to cope with the work load that I had taken on. I believe the Lord just set me aside."

Despite all this Joe still seems unable to say no as the invitations flood in. His ministry continues unabated throughout the year, although he has learned the wisdom of taking the whole month of July off every year, just to recharge the batteries, physically as well as spiritually.

13

A WIDER MINISTRY

"It's been lovely to be involved in the Lord's work over the years. For me it's been a great privilege to watch it develop and to know that I've been used of God in the extension of His kingdom on earth."

Since his own conversion Joe's been privileged to see many others come to the Saviour through his ministry, both in song, testimony and preaching. If he'd kept a case book it would have been filled many times over. He can recite examples by the handful.

"I used to sing and preach at a coffee bar in the Dungannon area called 'The Lighthouse.' One night, in 1985, I spoke to the young people on the necessity of being saved."

"Afterwards, a young man by the name of Stephen Mark came to talk to me. He was very troubled about his spiritual condition and after talking to him for a while I had the joy of leading him to the Saviour."

Stephen Mark's story doesn't end there. The Lord impressed upon him the need to reach the whole world with the gospel and Stephen decided to dedicate his life to the service of Christ. He went to Bible College and then, through the auspices of The New Tribes Mission, left for South America where he is in missionary service even today. Stephen still writes to Joe at least once a year and in each letter he reminds him of that night in Dungannon when Joe pointed him to Calvary.

YOUTH FOR CHRIST!

A couple of years ago Joe conducted a youth mission in Hillsborough. One night a big lad of nineteen got saved. He has developed well too and has just taken up a post as a trainee teacher in the Christian day school, in Portadown.

A young woman, eighteen years old, rang Joe at home one night in a terrible state of distress. She had attended some of his children's meeting years before but had never come to Christ. She went to work in a local office and there she met a few Christians who witnessed to her about her need of salvation. Remembering the man who had conducted the meetings for boys and girls, years before, she telephoned him. That night, over the phone, Joe led her to his Lord. She has never looked back. Truly, a case of 'casting your bread upon the waters.'

AUSTRALIA

Joe's ministry has taken him overseas as well. His son Mark was a missionary student at the Whitefield College of the Bible, in Laurencetown, near Lurgan. When his studies were completed he was asked to go out to Australia to assist the Rev. Michael Patrick, the minister there.

In due course an invitation came to Joe as well. Would he go out for a month and give the Australian believers a taste of his singing and preaching? How could he refuse?

During his stay meetings were arranged all over the place and Joe was kept busy singing the gospel and expounding from the scriptures. It was a welcome visit as far as the Rev. Patrick was concerned too. He got his first break in three and a half years as Joe conducted some of the Sunday services and looked after the prayer meetings as well.

It was a wonderful experience but one that Joe wouldn't want to repeat too often, unless there's some better means of transport invented. Joe just doesn't like flying! His prayer, when in the air, seems to be that of another well known Ulster cleric "Lord, let me be down and out."

"Have you ever done without sleep for thirty-seven hours? I did," says Joe. " I felt every bump in that aeroplane the whole way to Australia and the whole way back."

I CAN'T FLY!

But why should a saint of God who's going to a far better place be afraid of flying?

"Well it was fear - and that's just the natural response of the body. I don't mind sailing because if anything happens I can swim a little bit. But I can't fly at all and if anything happens up there in the air - I can't do a thing. I'm always very conscious that I'm so high up in the air. It's just something that's in-built and I just can't help it."

Well Joe Peden's not the first person to have an aversion to flying and he'll not be the last either. And after all, for someone, who has little experience of flying, to undertake a journey of such distance, flying almost all the way at night, is a considerable undertaking. And he has to be given credit for actually going through with it. He could have said no!

PRISON MINISTRY

Much nearer to home, much nearer to his heart and very firmly on terra-firma is Joe's ministry in the prisons. He has a great heart of compassion for those men who have been caught up in violence through what is referred to in Northern Ireland as 'The Troubles."

Joe has taken part in many services in the prisons of Northern Ireland, including some in Magilligan prison in the North West. The first time he arrived for a service in Magilligan he was rather unusually surprised. It had, of course, been announced that he would be there and when the prisoners gathered for the meeting, among them was one of Joe's former foot-balling colleagues. In fact he had been playing football on the day Joe had broken his leg. He hadn't seen him since then.

THERE BUT FOR THE GRACE OF GOD!

"This chap had, unfortunately, been caught up in one of the para-military organisations and was now serving a very long sentence. I felt very sorry for him. However, it was a great privilege to meet him again and to be able to tell him what the Lord had done for me and how he had changed my life. Who knows, but for the Lord's intervention in my life I could have been in the same situation."

"When I think about my past life and how bad things were when I was being destroyed by drink, I'm thankful that I never got caught up in any of the para-military organisations. I had the wisdom, when I was invited to join some of those organisations, to say no. When I look at some of the young men I see in the prison I think that I, too, could have been where they are. Just one wrong word would have been enough. However, the Lord in his mercy kept me out of all that and I have great cause to thank Him."

In fact Joe has met quite a few people he knows in the prison. Some are former workmates, some are from his football days and some are just friends and acquaintances. For them all he has an attitude of compassion and to them all he has the message of forgiveness and hope through the gospel. That message is well summed up in the words of the apostle Paul, in his famous and powerful sermon in the synagogue at Antioch. "And by Him (Jesus) all that believe are justified from all things, from which they could not be justified by the law of Moses." (Acts 13 v 39.)

Joe also goes into the Maze prison regularly where he sings and preaches to the prisoners. He can reel off a whole list of names of men who have become almost personal friends through his ministry to them. A good number of these men have found Christ in the prison cell and, while they must serve out their sentences in repayment of their debt to society, more importantly, they are serving the Lord in the prison.

INTO ALL THE WORLD

In the near future he also hopes to open up a correspondence ministry with a number of prisoners. Several of them have expressed the desire to write to Joe and have asked if it's O.K. with him. Joe, of course, is delighted at the prospect and has gladly agreed to be of whatever help he can. It has to be sanctioned by the prison authorities but, if it is, Joe will be putting pen to paper regularly in the hope of further encouraging and guiding those in prisons.

Another of Joe's interests, burdens if you like, is the work of missionaries in foreign countries. In support of this he has given freely of his services as a singer. Indeed, it has made him into a recording artist. But it's just another side to the man for whom no sacrifice is too great to make for the kingdom of Heaven.

The establishing of a Christian witness in any foreign country is a long and arduous task. Many are the hurdles, set backs and discouragements that have to be overcome. That's always been the case and it's hardly likely ever to change. Right from the times of William Carey, now referred to as 'the father of modern missions,' those who have left their homeland and loved ones, to preach the gospel in regions beyond, have had to battle against every conceivable form of Satanic opposition.

In the early days it was manifested in downright physical abuse and sometimes death. Many a foreign shore has been stained with the blood of God's most precious saints who have paid the supreme sacrifice in the service of their Lord.

Some have been stricken down by tropical disease, by venomous reptile or by marauding beast. Others have simply worn themselves out by service, day and night, to God and their fellow man.

In many a remote, unheard of little corner of the globe their bodies have been laid to rest and their bones lie awaiting the trumpet sound of resurrection. Forgotten by man they may be, but they are not forgotten by the Saviour. At that great day He will call them into His presence and with a welcoming smile declare "Well done, thou good and faithful servant."

MODERN PROBLEMS

In these latter times death, either by sickness or violence, is less probable. Modern medicine has taken care of the one. A shrinking world and the influence of nearby civilisations has made the other less likely. But still God's true servants suffer opposition. If Satan has one weapon of destruction wrenched from his grasp he'll soon find another.

Nowadays the modern missionary faces opposition from heathen religion that abhors the name of Christ. From the stringent legislation that operates in many lands, making entry into a country, just to preach the gospel, impossible or illegal. Or from the humanistic influences of scientists and anthropologists who claim that, to ask men and women to give up their heathen gods and practices and bow down to Jesus Christ, is to ask them to give up their native culture.

It's strange that those who make such claims on the behalf of native people set us no example.

They don't go about their daily business on foot, or on horseback, as Europeans did years ago. They don't cook on a wood fire. They don't read by candle-light. They don't travel to foreign lands, on their anthropological studies, in crude boats or sailing ships. They're very fond of the trappings of western civilisation and carry as much of it with them wherever they go.

However, for many years, the main difficulty facing the missionary has been lack of capital - hard cash. Local congregations continually face appeals from missionary societies for this or that piece of new equipment. In this age of affluence it's amazing that some missionary societies don't even have the money to support the missionaries they already have on the foreign field. They can't even contemplate sending out new people, so serious are the cash restrictions.

SUPPORT

For all these reasons missionaries need to be supported, as faithfully as possible, by those back home. In the Tandragee church, to which Joe Peden belongs, the members have a very strong sense of duty towards missionaries in general and towards one in particular.

Margaret Russell heard the call of God to missionary service and dedicated her life to that cause before she was out of her teens. She went to Bible college and studied hard. The vision of the African continent and Kenya, in particular, loomed before her and a few years ago, alone, she set sail to serve Christ amongst the people God had burdened her for.

Sadly, many who are sent forth, with a marvellous and emotional valedictory, to missionary service in a foreign land, are soon forgotten. The pressures, or perhaps the comforts, of home fade the memory and the lonely servant on a distant shore is as forgotten as yesterday's sunshine.

Such is not the case, however, with Margaret Russell. She's dear to the hearts of the people in Tandragee church. Never a week is allowed to pass without her name being mentioned and never a prayer meeting has a benediction pronounced without her and her work being lifted up at the throne of grace. They love her as dearly as if she were their own daughter - and in many ways she is.

KENYA

Some of the lads in Tandragee church got together a few years ago and put together a little recording studio. Their main purpose in doing this was to raise a bit of money which would be earmarked for the support of Margaret Russell's work in Kenya.

It was almost inevitable that Joe Peden would be roped in to help in this ministry and sure enough, one day, after he had sung at an open-air meeting, he was approached about making a recording. He readily agreed and after some weeks of hard work in the little studio at the back of the church, his first recording, a cassette of a dozen or so of his most popular gospel songs, was released.

"The first effort was fairly simple and basic. However, it took off and was reasonably successful. Sales of the tape went to quite high numbers. That inspired us to make a few more"

Joe's tapes did sell well and they generated a bit of cash, some of which was ploughed back into the studio, to improve the facilities and help them produce even better recordings. But more importantly, large amounts have been raised in support of the missionary cause in Kenya.

Even as this book is being written Joe is recording yet another album. This time it's being recorded in one of Northern Ireland's top professional recording studios and being released by one of the U.K.'s foremost recording labels. As well as being on cassette, as before, this new album will also be available on the modern compact disk format. That's something Joe's very excited about.

Again, the proceeds will go to further missionary effort in Kenya and that brings Joe the biggest thrill of all.

Early in his christian life he learned the words of Jesus 'Go ye into all the world and preach the gospel to every creature.'

He has gone, in person, all over Northern Ireland and the U.K., driving hundreds of miles. He has gone, in person, to Australia, braving a flight of thousands of miles. He can't travel everywhere, in person. But by his persistent efforts in his own country, his gospel recordings which have gone far and wide, and now this book, Joe Peden is doing what he can to obey and fulfil Christ's great commission. Those who know him well - will wish him well!

14

EPILOGUE

There's no doubt that Joe Peden's chief burden is for the youth of today. Earlier in this book he harked back to the one man, a school-teacher, who made the most significant impression upon him during his school days. He made that impression because he seemed to understand what being young is all about.

Joe Peden seems to have been endowed with that same ability - the ability to understand what's going on inside young heads, the ability to guide them in the right direction - and to do it without any degree of dogmatism or offence.

Over the years many young people have called at Joe's home asking to have a chat with him. He's always been there with a listening ear and a gentle, timely word of advice. As he's travelled throughout the country, too, he sat for many an hour with a group of young people gathered around him, just listening.

"When I look back on my own young days I have to admit that there are far more attractions and temptations for young people today. They are living in difficult days.

"I have sat and talked with young people in numerous churches. They just want someone to care for them, to listen to them. I believe that's where we're missing out today.

"However, it's not for me to tell them what they should and should not do, as Christians. I went through all this with the football and eventually, the Lord made clear His will for me. Nobody else told me. The Lord told me. I believe if a young man's going on with God and trying to please God in everything he does, God will show him what's right.

"It's my own view that older Christian people are far too demanding of young people. They tear young people to shreds, telling them how they should look, how they should live, what they should do and what they shouldn't do. In general, they're destructive rather than constructive.

"I believe we ought to sit down with young people, listen to them, learn to communicate with them and to understand them. We have to be able to talk with them, laugh with them and build up a relationship with them. Then we have some hope of making progress with them.

"We're anxious about young people after they've gone away out into the world but what have we done to hold on to them. That question can be asked of the church in general, of Sunday School teachers, of youth leaders, of mothers and fathers and of individual Christians."

"Oh God, give us all a burden for the youth!"